Ten Times
Round the Clock

Ten Times
Round the Clock

Behind the wheel with
New Zealand's leading motoring writer

Peter Gill

HarperCollins*Publishers New Zealand Limited*

First published 1999

HarperCollins*Publishers (New Zealand) Limited*
P.O. Box 1, Auckland

Copyright © Peter Gill, 1999

ISBN 1 86950 303 1

Designed and typeset by Graeme Leather
Printed by Griffin Press, Australia

Contents

Foreword

This book observes no rules.

Why? Well, it wasn't my idea in the first place. It came at a difficult time in terms of finding spare hours to write it.

It was the idea of the very kind publishers and their very kind associates.

It is written on my terms. Political correctness simply does not figure.

I appreciate the fact that you won't want to hang around too long. You love cars and driving. But right now you simply want to read for a bit, then go to sleep. Or maybe you have seen something somewhere about a quick way to the G-spot and you are keen to try it. So you don't want some hefty tome of a book to get in the way. Or you have already been down the road towards the G-spot and found the search party fairly expensive to hire, and now you want to spend a short time with something that will help you get off to sleep. Or maybe there's something on TV. Or your plane trip is fairly short. Or you are on hols.

Whatever, I am here to reward your investment, or the investment of the person who had the poor taste to buy you this book, by not holding you up for too long. Not holding folks up for too long has been the driving force of my writing style for around three decades. The technique was not even fashionable when I started in this game.

Thus the dedications will be short. The stories will be too. You will whistle through this book at fuel-injected and super-charged speed. The fact that you're still with me so far is a victory over the Internet, satellite TV, hired videos, CD-ROMs, the cinema, magazines and papers.

Right. Let's get on with it. The dedications, that is.

Dedication

To Anne, who has been hauled round the clock with me. She has long had to put up with having to change the seat and mirror adjustment every day because she is rarely in the same car two days running. Such are the rigours of the test programme. She provides opinion. She has had to put up with driving everything from a BMW 850 or a Jaguar Sovereign to a Daihatsu Charade or a Holden Barina. I sincerely apologise to her for the inconvenience.

To Les and Ruby, my parents, who trusted me to drive a car as a teenager without daily dire warnings. I appreciated that.

And to Rachel Gill, our daughter, who was not in this life long enough even to see a car, let alone to ride with us ten times round the clock.

To Neil Nelson and Steve With, fallen comrades.

And to my excellent TV News workmate of so many years, Tom Bradley, who phoned me one day and said, 'Peter, I think there is a book in you. I have a publisher.'

I was busy and did not need that call, and wished Tom had picked on someone else. But let me be honest. I have known many people who have tried to get a book published and have either not succeeded or have had to finance it themselves. Unlike me, they had not been made an offer by a publisher. Anne thought I should do it. Colleagues at the *National Business Review* and *New Zealand Driver* magazine thought the same. So I cancelled a chunk of my life to give it a try.

I think it is probably unusual in a dedication to refer to the publisher, but as this book observes no rules, no conventions, I wish to acknowledge HarperCollins New Zealand and their publisher Ian Watt for their indecently hasty and energetic faith in Tom's idea from the very start.

Oh, by the way. It is customary, fashionable and sexy to acknowledge those who have given the author shoulder massages, coffee or inspiration, or who have ceaselessly researched, typed and checked manuscripts. In that category I have no-one to thank, except perhaps Bill Gates, who sold me a halfway reasonable but by no means perfect word processing programme.

Position Statement

Question addressed by friends to my wife, Anne:

'Of all those borrowed cars crammed into your driveway, which is the best one?'

Answer: 'The one with the most gas in it.'

Prologue

It is October 1998. Today I drove a $500,000 car. It was a brand new Rolls-Royce Silver Seraph. It was the most expensive car I have ever driven. Rolls-Royce had earlier written to me to say that the Silver Seraph, the first all-new Rolls-Royce model in seventeen years, was now in production and one had been shipped to the New Zealand distributor. I therefore saw it as my duty to readers to find it and drive it.

So I walked into the showroom and asked for a drive. The sales people recognised me as the motoring writer from *National Business Review*, *Driver* magazine, *Sunday News*, and others . . . and agreed immediately to my request. Why beat about the bush? There is a certain amount of privilege that goes with this job. Like any privilege, the test of the privileged person is in how they handle themselves. The second you abuse a privilege, you will be cut down. And rightly so.

And so I drove this half-million-dollar car. I put kilometres on it that they did not really want put on it, because they wanted to sell this half-million-dollar car as genuinely new. But the fact that they were prepared to make an exception and to wear a few kilometres on the clock in order to indulge me was gratifying to say the least.

What is so special about that? The fact is that this is the first and only time in my career that I have *asked* for a test drive. Except this one, every car that I have test driven has been offered to me, sometimes even pressed on me.

The other thing that's special is that the Seraph is the most expensive car I have been entrusted to drive. This seemed somehow fitting in a week when I celebrated 30 years and a million kilometres of test driving, a week in which I went round the clock for the tenth time.

DETOUR

I have to admit I am verbally incontinent when it comes to extracting the urine. During this million-kilometre journey of 30 years, several editors of car magazines have encouraged the devilish side of my nature by publishing its product in their fine, glossy journals. The editor of *New Zealand Car* magazine for many years, the respected High Priest of motoring journalism Donn Anderson, was the first to foster this particular type of expression. Publishers Mark Petch of *New Zealand AutoCar* and Allan Dick of *New Zealand Driver* magazine have also shown their appalling taste by printing these outbursts. As I have always retained copyright to my own material, I am able to share abridged extracts with you. Those selected were first published by *New Zealand Driver*, the *National Business Review* and, in one case, *New Zealand Car* magazine when it belonged to Wilson and Horton. Each of those parties is thanked for their cooperation. These outbreaks will crop up here and there throughout the book, under the heading 'Detour'. The first of them appears on page 26.

First Car, First Girl

Show me the person who does not remember their first car. I am 49 years old as I write these words. Like most New Zealanders and Australians in my age group, my first car was quite old when I got it. I will never forget it, as I am sure you haven't forgotten yours. It embarrassed me in the eyes of the first girl I ever asked out. Cars did that kind of thing then. New Zealand was a car-starved nation. You needed a deposit in overseas funds to get a new car. If you had that, the car still cost you an arm and a leg, and perhaps the other leg too. My wife tells me I have short legs. I tell her the reason is that over the years finance companies have cut a little bit off each month in order for me to indulge myself with decent cars.

In the 1960s and 1970s, most young folk put up with recycled cars that were kept on the road by much reconditioning, refurbishing, mouth-to-mouth resuscitation and mechanical organ transplant surgery. New Zealand's cars were the joke of the world, and overseas visitors would lampoon us on account of their age.

During the Second World War, New Zealand and Australian soldiers were revered for the way they could resuscitate an ailing army vehicle. Wire, bandages, army hospital ether dropped into carbs — all these techniques amazed the Americans and the British.

This spirit of innovation survived through the '60s and early '70s. The conventional wisdom of those times was that to get a warrant of fitness for your ten- to twenty-year-old car it was prudent to take certain precautions. These included:

1. Blasting wheel bearings and kingpins chock full of grease on the day of the warrant test. This layer of grease between surfaces disguised wear.

2. Borrowing some wheels for an hour from a student mate whose car had the same size wheels and tyres as yours. This would equip your car with a full set of well-treaded and instantly warrantable tyres.

3. Wearing a tie when arriving for a WOF test and calling the mechanic 'Sir'.

So desperate were we to acquire the best car we could for the least amount of money, that as a seventeen-year-old I managed to appal even my mother. She was a strong supporter of my need to have a car, and helped me out with money. But one day I came home with a scheme to get myself a fairly flash Jaguar that nearly lost me that support. I had heard that a man had committed suicide in his Jaguar in Auckland's Waitakere Ranges. This unfortunate event was not discovered for a week or more, and the car was now being put up for tender. Unfortunately my mother issued a very strong directive, as a consequence of which there was no tender from Peter Gill.

It hadn't been a good week all round. A bunch of us teenagers had hatched a plan to tell our respective mothers that we had got a girl pregnant, just so we could enjoy the reaction.

We would later compare maternal reactions and what they registered on the Richter scale. It was not a good week to have mentioned the suicide Jaguar.

My first car was bought when I was at university studying for a degree at the expense of the New Zealand Broadcasting Corporation. The NZBC had me sit a creative writing test and then took me on directly from school as a cadet. I had cash in my pocket because the NZBC paid me while I studied.

The car was a 1951 Singer SM1500. It was a product of the original Singer company before they joined Rootes Group, after which their cars were badge-engineered Hillmans. It was over fifteen years old when I acquired it. It was maroon in colour, and it quickly became known as the red whale. Its silhouette certainly had the curves of a whale, and its sluggish handling and ride could perhaps also be compared to a whale.

It had one of those incredible column changes of that era, made of buff-coloured plastic that became sticky to the touch. The gear lever flopped and sagged like an atrophied limb hanging from the steering column. You didn't change gear. You entered a lottery. If you were a lucky winner, you found the gear you wanted.

Of course, on buying one's first car, one had to convince one's folks that it was a safe car, bought from a reputable seller, and that one could be trusted to own, drive and manage it without needing to make a reservation in the intensive care unit. Quite simply, I bullshitted my parents. I told them I had bought it from a priest. That was good enough for them. Reality is that the seller, for all I knew about him, may well have been a West Auckland axe murderer.

The acquisition of that car was the beginning of a process that was to characterise the rest of my life. About twice a year I would sell my car and get another, theoretically better, one. Among the early cars that I owned and nurtured as a student in the late 1960s was a 1954 Renault 750. I still have the handbook for it. It looked like a turtle, but its performance and handling

15

were vastly superior to anything British. This gave me a passion for European cars that has remained with me ever since.

The sheer perversity of the French was summed up in this car. Its fuel filler sat neatly above its rear-mounted engine, meaning petrol could drip almost directly onto the hot engine block. I found that idea novel in the extreme. This same perversity was still alive and well 35 years later, with the result that on the beautiful Citroën BX it was necessary to cancel the indicators manually. At the time Citroën was the only car company in the world that did not believe in self-cancelling indicators lest they cancelled before you wanted them to.

I owned a Renault again in the late 1970s, and loved it. It was a Renault 12, built at Thames on the Coromandel Peninsula in a factory that later became the Toyota assembly plant. It was an extraordinarily economical car, and by using excellent gear ratios it gave an impressive performance from its little 1200-cc engine.

In the early 1990s I saw what may well have been my old Renault 12, looking much the worse for being French. It still had a label on the rear bumper that said: 'If the French are so keen to have a bomb, they can have this one back.'

I only ever owned one Ford in that era, again during my student days. It was a Mark 1 Consul. I could scarcely believe how Ford got away with the windscreen wiper system it installed on Zephyrs, Consuls, Prefects and Anglias in the 1950s. Instead of having an electric motor, the wipers were vacuum powered. At low speeds there was plenty of vacuum available. But when you were accelerating or climbing a hill all the vacuum got bled away by the engine's automatic advance/retard mechanism and the wipers stopped. So there I was, hauling up towards the crest of the Auckland Harbour Bridge in a monsoon and suddenly I was blinded. Perhaps the teachers at secondary school had been right after all, I thought. But they had forgotten to say that the blindness would come on quite this suddenly. I eased off the gas pedal because I couldn't see a thing, and suddenly the wipers went into an eccentric fit, whacking back and forth so fast they were a veritable blur. Damned strange way to design a car, I thought. But as far as I know, all English Fords of the era had this system.

A stand-out car of my student days was a 1956 Armstrong Siddeley Sapphire 236. I was the only student at Auckland University to roll up to the carpark in something that looked as if it was built to cart the Governor-General around. Normally a nineteen-year-old student on a meagre allowance from the NZBC would have needed a good line in bank robbery to afford a luxury car such as this. The fact was that I bought it extraordinarily cheaply because it had met with a disaster or two. If you examined it at close quarters, this fact became obvious. Earlier that year, there had been a whirlwind that demolished a couple of buildings in the posh Auckland suburb of Remuera. The Armstrong had copped several low-flying pieces of debris, the results of which had been inexpertly panel-beaten out. But there's more. Someone had removed the cylinder head for mechanical repairs and somehow water had got into one of the bores of the lovely old straight six-cylinder engine. Presumably the car had been left in the rain with the bonnet up or off. When the engine was fired up after reassembly, the piston in the water-affected bore travelled upwards, as they do, and tried to compress the water. Water does not compress easily. The strain had to be taken somewhere, and it was the con rod that gave. The rod bent slightly, with the result that on each revolution it would touch the bottom of the bore. The car ran beautifully, but it gave off a loud clicking sound that resembled an industrial sewing machine. But wait. There's more. Somehow, some way, reverse gear had lost a tooth or two. The upshot of this was that when reverse was engaged the car would progress backwards in a series of indelicate bunny hops as a piece of the cog that still had teeth on it picked up drive. When the bald bit came round again, motion ceased. There's more. The car always smelt like a compost heap. One day I discovered toadstools growing out of the back carpet, just below where a window seal had been taking in rainwater.

I would have liked to have had everything fixed but it would have cost too much. Reluctantly I let the car go at the wooing of an Armstrong Siddeley enthusiast and mechanic. Off he went over the horizon, his crop of toadstools swaying in unison on the rear floor and the engine clicking madly like a flock of woodpeckers on uppers.

I missed that car badly. I loved Armstrongs dearly and wrote about them often in my columns. When Anne and I married in the 1970s, the Armstrong Siddeley Car Club provided two Sapphire limousines as wedding cars. Anne had to run around in her wedding dress with a milk bottle getting water for the one that arrived to pick her up from her home. Its radiator was running very hot. But the two Sapphires completed their task without letting us down.

Speaking of wooing, a little while ago I said that my first car embarrassed me in the eyes of the first girl that I asked out, Judith. I have a feeling that you will be expecting to know precisely what happened.

Well, she was vital. She was expressive. She was abundant. The girl, that is, not the car. She was a schoolmate and a neighbour. I had followed her progress with interest as at the end of our primary school years she burst into bud and then into full fruit.

I was seventeen and she was sixteen by the time I got the Singer. I made a date with her, arranging that I would pick her up at her place in the car. I got to her place and things were looking fine. Until the steering box on the Singer seized in her parents' driveway. Such a failure, and such a serious one, would be almost unheard of today. But in those days, the cars that we could afford were so old. I count myself lucky that the steering failed on someone's front lawn, not on a main road.

I learned three lessons from this:

1. That the Government policy that saw Kiwis given no choice but to drive old and clapped-out cars was something I would fight from that moment on. This was a safety issue as much as anything else.

2. That charity was alive and well in late-'60s New Zealand, in that Judith's parents allowed me to leave the stricken car on their front lawn for five days while I located a steering box from a wrecker's yard and brought it home on the bus wrapped in an old sack.

3. That there was no saving the romance. The guy up the road whose family owned the local sawmill had access to new cars. He stole her away forever in a brand new company-owned Mark 3 Ford Zodiac with new-fangled electric windscreen wipers.

The Bent Cars

It had to happen. In a million kilometres of test driving you would have to be going at a fair pace to be consistently ahead of Sod, the guy who drafted the law that took his name. True to say, then, that things have occasionally gone awry.

Metal has been bent in the cause of testing cars. Yet, fortunately, neither I nor anyone else involved has been injured. I have scars that would deify a returned warrior. I have scars that aficionados of the game snakes and ladders could play their intergalactic championship matches on. But they are all from mundane happenings such as slipping over on the ice while walking to school when I lived in Britain, or falling off the push-bike I owned in my adolescence. In one case, I was knocked off my bike on a main road near Whenuapai by an insurance salesman driving a blue Standard Ten. I was taken off to the air force hospital for yet another round of embroidery.

Three or four years later, as a licensed driver, I happened to buy a blue Standard Ten. It was one of the procession of cars I owned in my late teenage years. I got strange vibes from this car after I had owned it for a few weeks. It was trying to tell me something. I looked up some records and, sure enough, it was the car that had biffed me. Marks from where it had connected with my bike could still be seen. To its credit, the car ran very well for me. A dull little vehicle to look at, the Standard Ten clocked up several international rally successes in its time. It was the predecessor to the far more sporty Triumph Herald, a few of which can still be seen on the roads, mainly thanks to dedicated restorers and collectors.

Now a young cadet reporter with an interest in matters automotive, my body was about to suffer less, but the vehicle insurance industry was destined to suffer greatly, to the point where I may well be singularly responsible for the rocketing costs of insuring a car in New Zealand.

For a local TV magazine show, I had been sent to report on what was claimed to be the biggest truck certified for use on New Zealand public roads at that time. It had just been commissioned by the Auckland building materials company Winstone, to haul river sand from the Waikato to Auckland.

Executives of Leyland, the supplier of the truck, entreated me to get in and take it for a test drive around the Winstone yard. Unfortunately, my truck-driving experience was limited to the occasional drive of the Bedford fire engine belonging to the volunteer fire brigade of which I was a member. And so I did not take into account the fact that when cornering, the rear of a very long trailer will describe an arc that cuts deeper into the corner than that of the cab end of the rig.

The rear portion of the trailer collected a parked Triumph 2000 belonging to Leyland, and propelled it into a parked Chrysler Valiant belonging to someone from Winstone, which in turn was propelled into the wall of a shed. Once all the executives had regained their colour they were extraordinarily decent about the whole thing. For some reason my editors, however, decided not to include the incident in the TV programme.

I had another encounter with Sod one day while heading

towards the coastal town of Leigh, north of Auckland. Driving an Austin Princess, on a blind crest on a narrow road I came into a low-speed head-on collision with a Holden Kingswood. Neither Anne nor I were injured, so we freed ourselves and made in the direction of the other car. My eyes met those of the other driver as he strode across the road, and while we had made a fair mess of two cars, neither of us could resist a smile. The other driver was a former workmate of mine at the NZBC, Gordon Ell, who went on to become a leading light in the Forest and Bird Protection Society. We shook hands in the middle of the road and caught up on old times. No-one was hurt in his car either, although the incident was a tiny bit inconvenient, as at that particular moment he was leading a convoy of cars containing nature lovers on an outing to the nearby marine reserve.

Later, after retrieving parts of the Princess from a nearby field, I phoned Dauntsey Teagle, the well-known racing driver and executive with the New Zealand Motor Corporation, who had loaned me the car. I explained what had happened. 'No problem, Peter,' Dauntsey said. 'Get a tow truck and have the car brought back to us. Austin Princesses are much easier to sell to the insurance company than they are to customers. Come in on Monday morning and I'll have a decent car for you to test, a Honda Civic.'

When I wrote about the event in a newspaper column later I entitled it 'Death of a Princess', after a television documentary Prime Minister Rob Muldoon would not allow to be shown here. The documentary was about some kind of ritual sacrifice of an Arab princess, and Muldoon thought that showing it would upset relations with our main oil suppliers. Who would have thought that fifteen or so years later I would be asked to write a story on another car accident, a much more prominent one, for which the title 'Death of a Princess' would also be apt.

When the huge Mercedes Benz S Class was released I had test driven several examples in France for a few days at a time. I felt compelled to say in my story that if I had to choose a car to have a bad crash in, the Mercedes Benz S Class would be on my shortlist. It is an extraordinarily safe car. But when a moving object hits an immoveable one at maybe 150 km/hr, no car can guarantee to save its occupants. Princess Diana's heart was literally wrenched from its connecting vessels by the forces of deceleration.

While I was driving the huge S Class through the narrow and congested streets of Monte Carlo as part of a lengthy test drive, I made an error of judgment and one of its exterior mirrors snatched off the exterior mirror of a police Alfa Romeo coming the other way. I asked the Australian motoring writer who was travelling with me what he thought I should do. 'Boot it, mate,' said the gravelly Australian. 'The cop'll be ages trying to find enough space to do a U-turn and chase us.' I took his advice, and we didn't see the Alfa Romeo again.

On another occasion, again in the cause of doing a story for a TV magazine programme, the long-suffering New Zealand Motor Corporation offered me a drive of the Rolls-Royce they were to supply the Government for an upcoming visit to New Zealand by Queen Elizabeth II, alias Mrs Betty Windsor. While I was driving through the streets of Auckland, the temperature gauge shot up. Steam began to emanate from the slats in the world's most expensive grille. We had boiled Mrs Windsor's motor.

The Roller was carted off to Roller Hospital for some urgent attention. As far as I know it later managed to perform its royal duties without incident, although I noted that the tour organisers always had a Ford LTD or two tailing the convoy — presumably so that they could quickly rescue Betty should the Roller decide to go very British and pack a silver-plated sad.

At least the Roller gave me warning that something was up by sending the needle on the gauge soaring. The $100,000 Mazda 929 loaned to me in 1993 by Mazda New Zealand chief Peter Aitken did not. As the car climbed towards the crest of the

Auckland Harbour Bridge, it got slower and slower. My pilot training has disciplined me to scan instruments when things are going wrong, as well as to scan them even when things appear to be going right. There was not a single warning light on, nor any kind of contraindication anywhere. Being surrounded by traffic, I could not simply stop. The car was now hardly moving, but it limped over the crest, whereupon the engine died. I coasted down the other side and out of the way of the traffic.

Investigation proved that the 24-valve twin-cam 3-litre V6 engine had completely seized as a result of overheating. I asked Mazda's long-time and learned technical manager, Roger Russell, why I had not received a signal on the dash. The reason, said Roger, was the way in which the event occurred. The bottom radiator hose had come off at one end, having missed out on a securing clip in the factory in Japan. A combination of gravity and the still-turning water pump would have seen every drop of water fall onto the road in mere seconds. The sensor for the water temperature warning on this car is designed to measure and react to the temperature of the water — when there is no water to measure the temperature of, it does nothing. And so the boss came to lose his brand-new car.

Learner drivers are prime targets for Sod's Law. When I was attempting to teach Anne to drive, she was involved in a potentially serious incident with an oncoming BP road tanker. Not quite trusting my skills, she also had another tutor, with whom a less serious incident occurred which reportedly involved a rotary clothesline. Less serious, that is, unless you were an aficionado of rotary clotheslines and HB Vauxhall Vivas.

In some tight manoeuvring while learning to do a three-point turn using the safe haven of a lawn, Anne collided with the clothesline, which reportedly ended up looking like a giant sunflower, its huge round head nodding at the sun from atop its quivering stalk. The HB Vauxhall Viva, a model which possessed some very perverse curves and bends as part of its original design, was somewhat re-styled as a result. I doubt if anyone would have noticed, though. Fancy using HB, a designation created for pencils, to describe a car.

Anne also owned one of the earliest Honda 50 Stepthroughs to come to this part of the world. She got on well with that, apart from an incident in which she changed straight from fourth gear to first, and pitched herself and her friend over the handlebars, to the amusement of the occupants of a passing bus. Fortunately there were no lasting injuries.

After that she went on to become a staff member of the New Zealand Automobile Association, in a job that required her to teach others to drive. Apart from the occasional fender-bender that visits upon us all, there have been no further incidents. In my view, some time soon she should apply to take the driver's licence test.

DETOUR

I have always wondered just what, precisely, I am meant to do when I come up behind a car with a sign swinging away in the back window which announces: 'Baby On Board'. Do the displayers of these signs think that I scream around among the speed cameras killing adults, but that somehow my killer instinct dissolves into instant compassion when I learn that there is a 'Baby On Board'?

Do they think that I would happily kill THEM, but because of the sign, I would be sure to spare the baby? Are they asking me to back off and open up a three-kilometre protective zone between my front bumper and their tail pipe?

One such baby-on-boarder that I encountered kept her Honda sitting at precisely 40 km/hr, and hard on the centreline at that. It was only because she had her ears pierced that I could see when to overtake safely. Or are the baby-on-boarders simply bragging about their fertility? (Oh dear, Mum coughed at the wrong time and we're going to have to go out and buy another 'Baby-On-Board' sign. Mum can hang it round her neck for nine months then we'll hang it in the back window of the used import.)

There's only one sign more ridiculous than 'Baby On Board', and that's 'Show Dogs On Board'. Oh, and don't forget 'Want To Lose Weight? Stop Me And Ask How'. That one is amazingly effective at 100 km/hr. Then there was the Mitsubishi Chariot with Mum and five completely unrestrained kids romping and playing leapfrog all over the seats, the back window displaying a sign saying 'Jesus Saves'. He would need to.

3

Of Bikes, Bluebirds and Brassieres

It is ten past four on a summer afternoon at Whenuapai, north-west of Auckland. The year is 1964. I am a school kid with a bike. Not a multi-geared bike. Just a pre-owned direct chain drive bike that an RNZAF engineer has breathed magic on, and sold freshly painted to our family for three pounds. It was good value at that.

The air force guy, one Ozzie Johnson, gave it a lifetime guarantee. And he honoured it. He had to, really, living at the air base and being of junior rank. If he was going to trade in bikes and bike repairs on the side, and if some of his clientele were senior to him, he had to offer the world's best bike sales and repair service. And, as it happens, he did.

The bike that my father bought from bike charmer Ozzie Johnson, who had built it up from several wrecks, was the symbol of my independence. So now, at ten past four on this summer afternoon, I am enjoying one of my favourite occupations. I have propped up my Ozzie Johnson bike against a shed. I am wandering among the cars in the carpark of Auckland's International Airport. In 1964 Whenuapai is both an air force base and an international airport; I live here because my father is a member of the air force.

The cars I am wandering among represent the crème de la crème of what wealthier New Zealanders were driving in 1964. The cars are parked here because their owners have flown off in a Vickers Viscount, Lockheed Electra or Douglas DC4. At this time we are still a car-starved nation. There are massive restrictions on the importation of cars. Most ordinary Kiwi workers cannot aspire to ownership of a new car. Doctors, farmers and company directors can. They are exempt from the restrictions.

But ordinary Kiwis are required to stump up with a deposit in overseas funds. So only those with parents or grandparents in the old country who have given or left them money can aspire to a brand new Anglia with a notchback rear window for about 700 quid.

Most of us continued to breathe life into old cars. That year our next-door neighbour in the air force housing estate was driving a 1932 Essex Super Six. The sergeant across the road was doing slightly better. He had a 1951 Austin A40 Devon finished in a classy excrement brown. He also had three daughters who broke out into bud before my very eyes. I think it was following the progress of the ripening of this trio that gave me a lifelong fascination with the design features of the brassiere.

Anyway, every Saturday this air force sergeant would spend three hours hosing and sluicing his A40. Much of his effort was concentrated on dislodging dirt from under the wheel arches, thus preventing the onset of the greatest enemy of those times, rust. Here was a man who helped look after the air force's Bristol Freighters and De Havilland Devons. So he must have known something. Therefore, when he ambled across the road to give me advice on how best to clean my father's 1954 Hillman Minx, I listened.

He also gave me the impression, without saying so in as

many words, that if I laid as much as a quivering finger on any one of those three statuesque, dark-haired, female fruits of his loins I could confidently expect to be strangled with the afore-mentioned brassiere.

The family three doors along also had an outbreak of fragrant and understanding daughters. This airman drove a 1939 Chev, which I was frequently invited to climb aboard with the family for an outing to a nearby beach.

These people were reasonably well-paid servants of the Defence Department. Yet the ancient cars they drove were considered the norm. I can only think that governments of the time were still in postwar shock. They had no idea how the future of our nation would shake down, so they decided that continuing wartime rationing was the safest thing to do. And so everyone felt quite normal driving a car that was 20 or 25 years old. Can you imagine that now? Can you imagine relying on a car as old as that for your daily transport?

Anyway, back to my meanderings through the airport carpark. This is where I developed my interest in cars. They were showcased for me by the hundred, every day. No-one was worried that a kid wearing brown plastic sandals was eyeing up the cars in the airport carpark. These were gentler days. The biggest worry was that after a mere seven minutes of contact with human skin the plastic sandals smelt like the rottenest of rotten eggs. No-one worried about security. At that time the word denoted the 2s 6d in the pound, or some such sum, that people paid to ensure they got cradle-to-grave care under a scheme that was labelled 'Social Security'.

No-one was worried that this kid was snooping around people's cars and wandering around the airport terminal. In fact, they organised for the kid to be taken on board and shown around a Comet Four and a Bristol Britannia, and to be taken to the control tower. Not surprisingly, I developed a deep and abiding interest in aviation, and went on to become a private pilot.

How grateful I am for a childhood in which adults — all sorts of adults, not necessarily those known to my parents — simply said: 'Would you like to have a look on board this plane?' Sadly, today any adult making a perfectly genuine offer like that runs the risk of being regarded with suspicion. I have felt this pressure myself when I've been out for a run and some kid has wanted to engage me in chat and show me their new bike. I feel there are eyes behind curtains looking at me as I take an interest in whatever the kid has to say. I carry on with the chat, though, because I remember how good everyone was to me as a child. And to cave in to that kind of pressure just may be a reaction to perception rather than reality. And if the pressure is real, then the first person who bows to it hands victory to a whole new industry.

Anyway, back to the cars that were parked at the airport in 1964. That was when I saw my first Japanese car. The war had been over for eighteen or nineteen years at the time. Japanese products were not popular with everyone; it was the convent-ional wisdom to dismiss them out of hand, to make deprecating comments about how they copied British products (and they did), and to add the final insult by declaring that they were 'tinny'.

All kinds of redneck stories circulated. They talked of being able to read the name Mobil on the insides of the doors on Japanese cars — the implication being that they were made of old oil drums. This was the sort of arrant nonsense that can attach to any society that is being asked to accept cultural change. Quite simply, it is not possible to manufacture sheet steel from scrap in such a way that old markings could survive.

I would often hover around a frequent resident of the airport car park — a car called the Prince Gloria. It may be that the gender confusion wrapped up in this piece of nomenclature went right over my head at the time, so stunning was the car. The Prince Motor Company had designed a car that looked every bit as appealing and substantial as an American Rambler or Studebaker of that time. What's more, it had a 2-litre six-cylinder overhead camshaft engine and a DeDion-type rear axle. In other words, the Prince Gloria was not only stylish and fashionable, its mechanical underpinnings were by no means stolen from a museum. I read at the time that this was the first Japanese car to be promoted heavily in Europe, where the brand was debuted at the 1957 Paris Motor Show. By 1966, the engine of the Prince Gloria had been increased in size to 2.5 litres, and those who were prepared to consider Japanese cars on their merits instead of ritually slating them as being 'Jap crap' and 'tinny', were finding that the Prince Gloria had the ride and handling qualities of a Mercedes Benz. The Prince Motor Company was absorbed into Nissan not long afterwards, and that company continued to use some of Prince's design principles as well as its Gloria and Skyline model names.

There was another car that I beheld in that carpark that stood out from all the British Zephyrs, Zodiacs, Humbers and Vauxhall Veloxes. It was a boxy little four-door sedan labelled 'Datsun Bluebird'. In daring and brash gold script, the like of which I had never before seen, were fashioned the words 'full synchro'. What a wonderful thing this must be, I thought. My father constantly excused his many 'crunchy' gear changes in the 1954 Hillman Minx with the assertion that 'the synchro mesh is buggered'. This synchro thing was obviously a big deal. I checked into it. To change gear cleanly and successfully, and without graunch, it is necessary for cogs to be spun up to operating speed before meeting and engaging. If everything is turning at a similar speed, it will engage and marry fairly easily. Most British cars of that time did not offer synchronisation on first gear. This little Japanese car did. I was too young to drive myself, but I quickly deduced that what 'full synchro' meant was that you could slow down for a traffic light and drop into first gear with nary a hint of a graunch or a baulk. It was then that I knew the Japanese would have a serious impact on my later years.

I turned fifteen. My father gave me some driving lessons in the 1954 Minx, and his patience was rewarded by the fact that I took very little time to gain skills and confidence. In time, I presented myself to what was then known as a traffic officer for a driver's licence test. And so the journey began that was to take me ten times round the clock on behalf of my readers.

DETOUR

Welcome, ladies and gentlemen, to the induction course for new recruits to the road repairing industry. In this part of the curriculum I will teach you some handy tips for stopping motorists from becoming complacent.

Any roadworks sign, complete with 30 km/hr speed limit, should be erected at least three days before you plan to move to the site in question and start work. Similarly, you should leave it there for at least a fortnight after you have completed the job. Do not concern yourself about the sign falling over in the wind and blocking the roadway. It is just as effective in this position as it is when upright. You see, it keeps drivers on their toes . . . and their brake pedals.

Now to the matter of orange cones. In any line of orange cones that you establish, ensure that one — and one is sufficient — sticks out from the rest by about a metre, into the path of oncoming traffic. When you have done this, you will be able to observe how this technique stops motorists from speeding through roadworks with gay abandon. Oh, you can't use the word gay any more to denote happiness and fun, can you? Note that I have picked myself up on that one, ladies and gentlemen, because political correctness is very important in the roadworks game.

If you put up a sign saying CAUTION, WORKMEN AHEAD, please be sure that your gang consists only of men. We have been taken to the Human Rights Commission for less. If there are women in your work gang, and there often are today, please erect a sign that says EQUAL OPPORTUNITIES ROAD REPAIR PERSONS AHEAD.

And finally, when you have laid new gravel on wet tar, do not attempt to sweep the loose stones off the roadway. It is a waste of time and effort. You will find that the traffic moving through over a period of a couple of weeks will do that for you.

Watch what a shower of stones the average car kicks up in this situation. It is spectacular. We estimate that for every hundred cars passing through, one windscreen will be broken, but this seems a small price for the motorist to pay to have the roads maintained; and besides, isn't that what insurance is for?

Of Foreigners, Fast Cars, and Too Much Smoked Salmon and Chardonnay

Several times a year a gang of heavies will come around, abduct me and take me to Auckland International Airport, force me into a business class seat, pour Chardonnay down me for hours on end, frogmarch me into a luxury hotel suite in some foreign city, make me drive smart new cars for several days in exotic places, and then send me home in the same style.

At least that's the way it must sound to people when I frequently complain about the amount of overseas travel involved in being a motoring writer.

It is probably not all that well known to the readers of motoring columns and car magazines that on most occasions when one is invited to attend the launch of a new model, the car companies provide the air tickets, hotel accommodation, food and sometimes even entertainment. Most publications don't tell you about that part when they publish a story about their experiences test driving the brand new 3-litre quadcam Fiasco in the Swiss Alps, or even in Masterton, New Zealand.

I hasten to add that not every publication in the world accepts these offers.

But in the context of a major new product launch to the media, the journalist and his or her publication is asked to pay only personal and incidental expenses along the way. Travel, accommodation and meals are generally the car company's expense.

A perfectly legitimate question now arises. Does accepting travel and accommodation compromise the journalist in any way? Does he or she feel the need to say favourable things about the car and overlook some of its deficiencies? In my view, younger, less mature journalists can certainly have difficulty maintaining balance. To be whisked off in the business class cabin to Frankfurt, Paris, Tokyo or Detroit, and treated like a king for a week on someone else's tab, must unbalance the minds of some who are not yet used to it.

But I believe that with maturity comes an objective outlook that no amount of travel, smart hotels, smoked salmon and Chardonnay can puncture. It is an outlook that is a product of having seen and driven hundreds of cars, visited scores of factories, spoken to hundreds of designers, engineers and marketers, flown millions of air miles, and returned home utterly shagged for the next ten days.

There are reasons why the car companies shell out to get us there and back. Firstly, very few publications would have the budget to attend every model release. To get coverage, the car companies pay to get writers to the event. Secondly, if publications were to pay for travel and accommodation, there would be writers staying in all sorts of doss houses all over the place. With up to 800 journalists from all round the world attending some of the larger events, the car companies would lose control. They would not be able to round everyone up and get them all to the place required by the time required. By booking and paying, the car companies know precisely when everyone is arriving and can meet them, and they also know where everyone is staying so that instructions can be distributed as to where to be at what time.

I estimate that easily half of the world's motoring writers are freelance and therefore self-employed. Unlike a salaried person, they are not being paid while they are at such an event. Their only payment will be for the story they sell to a publication. Therefore, apart from payment for that story, they are completely unable to earn any other income because they are away from their office for a week, possibly longer.

I have known motoring writers at major metropolitan newspapers in New Zealand who are salaried staff members in other jobs at the papers, but are required to use their annual leave to attend overseas motoring events. Their motoring writing is considered completely secondary to their other jobs with the newspapers. The papers pay neither their travel and accommodation nor any of their time. These same papers eagerly publish the material and photographs generated by these journalists, and suck many millions of dollars a year out of the automotive sector by way of advertising revenue.

When some of these factors are considered, you can see how it becomes easier for motoring writers and their editors to accept travel and accommodation.

Sometimes the car companies do not realise how physically taxing the attending of events in Europe or Scandinavia can be for us Kiwis and Aussies. No-one else must fly for as many hours just to get there. Those from the UK and European countries might fly for one or maybe two hours. By the time we arrive, we could well have been on the go for up to 36 hours, only to find that the 1000-km test drive that will circumnavigate Germany twice starts tomorrow morning at 7 a.m. sharp. Ent you vill bee there. Heff you any qvestionz?

Dear reader, I can hear you saying, 'Oh dear, how sad, you

poor thing,' knowing, as you do, that you would just love to trade places with me and that you would be able to cope with anything just to go to exotic places to test drive new cars and not have to pay for anything. My reaction to that is a simple wry smile.

Typical of such events was the release in 1991 of the Mercedes Benz S Class, now in Mark 2 form. The business sessions were held in huge white marquees on the edge of the Mediterranean at Cannes. There was a two-hour briefing on the car's design features. You were given a headset that allowed you to listen to this briefing in any of five languages, thankfully including English. A squad of translators sat in glass fishbowls and gave running commentaries on everything that was said. Then they paired us off and issued each pair a new S Class.

We were to drive via Monte Carlo to Geneva. There were detailed instructions as to who to hand the car over to when we got to our hotel on the shores of Lake Geneva. We had to be certain we gave the keys to a genuine Mercedes Benz representative. The reason, we were told, was that at a Porsche media launch some months earlier some Mafia people had posed as carpark attendants and accepted keys from exhausted journalists as they completed their test driving for the day. According to one report at least three Porsches were spirited away by The Mob and have not been seen since.

Occasionally, I have played a trick on the car companies. Halfway between one big European city and the next, I have picked up the car phone they often issue us with in case we get lost or have trouble, and asked for instructions on 'how to repack these airbags'. When I did that on a major launch in the south of France one day, they sent a helicopter. So I have given up that little joke.

The launch of the BMW Seven Series was run out of Frankfurt. I was teamed up with broadcaster and colleague Allan Dick, who has been writing about cars for decades and is now publisher of *New Zealand Driver* magazine. Allan and I had thoroughly tested the Seven Series Sedan in a gruelling day's driving, so we cadged an Eight Series twelve-cylinder coupe and tried that for size. It was a six-speeder.

It would be stating the obvious to say it was an awesome experience. On a sunny day, in light traffic on a German auto-bahn that stretched to the horizon, Allan and I made a decision. We wanted to see 250 km/hr come up on the speedo.

The car's momentum slowly increased. 180. 200. Brief doubt. Should we continue this? 230, 240 and very gently . . . yes, there it was . . . 250 km/hr. This was about 80 km/hr faster than the speed the training planes at my flying club cruise at. We held it for a few seconds, knowing that the car was factory-governed to about that speed and would soon begin to falter. Just then two huge touring bikes of some description PASSED US.

Do not take this as advice to those intending to drive in Germany because we may have got it wrong, but it was very much our impression that the German authorities were not greatly bothered about speed limits, provided conditions were suitable, you were driving competently and, importantly, you were in a vehicle capable of handling high speed. I repeat, do not come round and throw stones on my roof if you try it yourself and get pulled up.

Twenty-five years earlier Allan and I had test driven together at the media launch of two quite different new models. What awful cars they turned out to be. They were the Austin Tasman and Kimberley. They were designed and built by the now defunct, and deservedly so, Leyland Australia. Leyland was desperately keen to break the stranglehold that Ford and Holden had on new car sales in Australia and New Zealand, so they created an artless, shapeless, soulless box on wheels based on the concept of the old Austin 1800 front-wheel-drive Land Crab.

In those days, the release of a new model was big news. So when a traffic policeman caught up with us on the Desert Road in the central North Island, claiming we were doing 90 miles an hour, Allan, even then considerably older and wiser than me, 'handled things'.

My memory of events was that the officer was driving a Hillman Hunter, but Allan thinks it was a Mark 4 Zephyr. Whatever, I vividly recall that you could smell this patrol car. The odour was a blend of hot engine, hot clutch, and hot, rusty radiator water. Clearly, he had been working this car very hard in order to catch up with us. As the officer approached us, banging and spitting noises emanated from the idling patrol car.

The officer got out his ticket book and wrote down the registration number of our test car. Then he went to write down the model of the car. Nowhere on it did there appear a model name. Leyland had removed all the badges and had taped bits of cardboard over parts of the car because it wished to keep as many details as possible secret until public launch day, which was still some way off.

'What is the make and model of this car?'

'We are not allowed to tell you,' said Allan.

Whereupon he wove an intriguing tale about this secret model, and how we would get into severe trouble with the manufacturer for breaking their cover, and possibly lose our jobs. The officer became very interested and started looking round the car. Allan said he would even give him a little drive if he promised to keep the matter a secret until the car was launched onto the market. The officer's demeanour softened considerably and then melted completely. We got away with a written warning.

Apart from test driving and specific product launches, the other events that some of us attend fairly frequently are motor shows in places such as Tokyo, Frankfurt, Amsterdam, Detroit and Geneva. Usually, the host is a car company that is debuting a new model at the show, but of course one is perfectly free to look at every other manufacturer's offerings at the show, and hosts expect that. After the show, you may be taken to a proving ground and invited to test drive your host's new models.

Quite the most fantastic track facility I have ever seen is a place called Twin Ring Motegi. Three hours' drive north of Tokyo, Honda has moved mountains and filled valleys to create a breathtaking track facility. Its epicentre is a 2.4-kilometre banked oval upon which I test drove the 1998 Accord. Whooping and hooping around, over and under this circuit is a 3.4-kilometre Grand Prix circuit which can be broken down into two short circuits. There is a kart track, a speedway track, a skid-pan area and a braking test area. All this takes up the area of a small town, and in fact it is a small town. Hotels have been built facing the track for the many motor sport enthusiasts who attend the various events there. There are corporate boxes, mobile caravan parks and shops, all set in a forested valley miles from anywhere and anyone. The cost of this development was not disclosed, but Motegi was completed at the beginning of 1998, just before the Asian economy began to feel chill winds.

As well as test driving the Accord, I was invited to do a few laps in a small single-seater racing car which Honda called the 'Side By Side'. The term derives from the fact that the car's 750-cc V-twin motorcycle engine is mounted beside the driver to give perfect balance. The car is designed for people learning to drive racing cars, but there is also a national championship competition based around it.

It has a five-speed sequential gearbox. You tug backwards on the cockpit wall-mounted lever to change up, and nudge forward to change down. The cockpit was fairly cramped and I kept knocking my elbows on the sides, rather restricting my steering action. But the little car had razor-sharp reactions and laser-accurate steering. It looked like a racing car too. My colleague Allan Dick felt that it fitted somewhere between a go-kart and a Formula Ford, which I thought was an astute observation.

Still in Japan, the Tokyo Motor Show is legendary for the way it has totally ignored the world trend away from draping mini-skirted women over cars. At this show, seemingly thousands of Japanese models in bright uniforms and heavily shrunken skirts parade hectares of nylon-encased leg flesh.

If you go to take a picture of a car, one of these nymphettes will twitter, smile and jump right into your shot. She thinks that's what you want.

Journalists can get hundreds of colour pictures on CD-ROMs, transparencies or prints on press day at the motor show. The car companies simply give them to you. You can collect so many pictures and press kits they are impossible to lug home. So the show organisers have a freight depot. You take your haul there. They put it into a large courier box and send it off to your home address at no cost to you or your publication. Lo and behold, it beats you home. Your personal luggage may get lost by the airlines, but your product information courier box never gets lost, and it travels faster than you do.

At the Tokyo Show, all that you are required to do to get these gorgeous CD-ROMs and pictures with which to decorate your feature stories and columns is pass over a business card. The twitterers do not look at the card at this point. They simply want to have received a card. Then you can have anything you like. If you have run out of cards, they are equally happy for you to write your details on a slip of paper. Later, when the show is over, they go through all the journalists' cards and slips and enter the details on a database. From that day forth you will be deluged with hundreds of press information parcels in the mail. It's a bit like *Reader's Digest* getting hold of your name and address. You will never get rid of them.

When I have finished looking at the cars I like to go to the truck and bus pavilion. I like to sit in the cabs of all the big rigs, the hearses, the ambulances, the street sweepers. As I am partial to writing the odd feature on heavy vehicles, I go up to the twitterers and ask for the pictures and the CD-ROMs. But what I do not want is to receive several thousand tonnes of press information directly from Hino and Isuzu on their latest city buses for the rest of my life. I appreciate that the more paper I receive from Japan the higher our export sales of timber pulp are likely to be. But I just can't handle the quantities of stuff they pump out. So I make out that I have run out of cards and offer the twitterers the also-acceptable slip of paper, which they take, but do not read at the time. On that slip of paper is written 'Fidel Castro, Havana, Cuba'. The bearded, cigar-smoking one must wonder why he keeps getting huge heaps of press brochures and photos of Japanese buses, fire engines, hearses, ambulances and street sweepers. But I would like to think that he enjoys them and finds them useful.

DETOUR

It's about time I had some recognition for my decades of cease-less service to motoring journalism. After all, was it not *moi* who pointed out to you years ago when Lada jokes were common that a Lada joke is not something you tell or hear? It's something you drive.

Was it not *moi* who pointed out to you that the Aussies have completely pulled the merino over the eyes of their countrymen by convincing them that the Commodore is an Australian car? The Commodore is a modified German Opel. Always has been. But then the Aussies do some pretty strange things. It was they who visited upon an unsuspecting market the Tasman, Kimberley, Nomad, Elite and P76. What's that, I hear you say? You've never heard of the Austin Nomad? Well, it was a sort of Austin Maxi with liposuction — it had no bum. No friends, either.

Anyway, recognition for my good works has finally come. I have been appointed chairman of the Move Right Commission. As you know, New Zealand and Australia are to change over from driving on the left-hand side of the road to driving on the right on February 4th, 2012. Sweden successfully achieved it in 1967. The Transtasman Move Right Commission has been tasked with making this transition successfully. We have already put much planning in place. Our thinking currently goes something like this:

> In Week One, buses will change over.
> In Week Two, trucks will change over.
> In Week Three, motorcycles will change over.
> In Week Four, cars and station wagons will change over.
> In Week Five, all remaining vehicles will change over.

The indigenous peoples of the land, under the Treaty of Waitangi, may change over if and when they feel like it. For more information phone 0800 LANE-CHANGE, or visit our website: www.mayhem.co.nz.au

In the public interest, any person who feels that he or she cannot adapt to the change will forfeit their car altogether. Compensation will be paid.

Our researchers have already identified several at-risk groups, who will almost certainly have difficulty with the change. These are the drivers of Isuzu Piazzas, Subaru Vortexes/ Vortices, Austin Montegos and anyone with a Personalised Number Plate. There will be a nationwide amnesty on all these cars. They will be crushed at designated crushing places. Post-crushing counselling will be available. For further information dial 0800 YEE HAH.

The Human Icons

It is sad, one could almost say negligent, that one of New Zealand's most famous sons has no memorial shrine in his own country.

One of the first assignments I was given as a fresh-faced teenage cadet news reporter with the NZBC was to cover the funeral of Bruce McLaren.

I had never met McLaren. He grew up in West Auckland as I did, but many years before me. In 1958, after showing great promise in New Zealand as a racing driver, he went to England. He was just twenty years old.

He raced a Cooper Climax in Formula Two events in Britain and Europe and was taken on by the Cooper factory team, the leader of which was Jack Brabham. Bruce McLaren won the 1959 United States Grand Prix, the 1960 Argentine Grand Prix, the 1962 Rheims Grand Prix and the Monaco Classic. The Cooper cars were becoming less competitive, however, and in 1965 McLaren left the team and formed his own. By 1968 he was using Ford Cosworth engines and had created cars that were highly competitive. He won the Belgian Grand Prix and finished fifth in the world championship. In 1970, at the age of 32, he died in a testing accident.

Bruce McLaren's body was flown home to Auckland and the funeral service was held in the Anglican Cathedral there, with his helmet on top of the casket. In Henderson, West Auckland, there is a road and a school named after him. But this appears to be the limit of his country's recognition of one of the great New Zealand names in international motor sport. I guess the fact that the McLaren name lives on as a racing car stable provides a living memorial, which is perhaps the best kind.

In the 1980s I did have the privilege of meeting McLaren's friend and team-mate Denny Hulme. After several famous victories, Hulme became world champion in 1967. For the next few years he went on to win Grand Prix after Grand Prix, finally hanging up his helmet in 1974. He took up saloon car racing after that. Sadly, he died at the wheel of a saloon car in a race in Australia in 1992, not of a crash, but of a heart attack. The car coasted harmlessly to a halt.

Denny was self-effacing, modest, and had a canny way of making you feel important when you were in his company. The third racing driver of the great New Zealand trio of that era, Chris Amon, has a very similar demeanour. Chris won many international events but could never quite get his hands on the World Championship. Over the years that Toyota assembled cars in New Zealand, Chris Amon designed modifications to their ride and handling to suit New Zealand's coarse chip roads and hilly geography. Toyota then built these modifications into the Japanese-designed cars.

Having met and been extremely impressed by the gentlemanly qualities of both Amon and Hulme, I can only surmise that their friend and fellow Kiwi Bruce McLaren would have exuded a similar aura.

I am not sure whether these men would agree with me, but I think Formula One racing has lost its character. It has become a battle as to who can throw the most money at developing a faster car rather than a battle of driving skills. There is also a disturbing propensity for the occasional driver to deal out a dirty trick such as a nudge here or a cut-in there. This is doubtless the result of the pressure of knowing how much money they are riding on and how much money is riding on them. As a result, I do not sit up half the night watching the races on television anymore.

Motorcycle racing, while also backed by big money, seems to me to be much more of a sporting challenge and far more exciting to watch. The international successes of the likes of speedway rider Ivan Mauger and track racer Aaron Slight have seen New Zealand well represented on two wheels.

I was once lucky enough to spend a day being taught driving skills by three-times world champion Jackie Stewart, who gave motor racing away as a profession because he had seen too many friends barbecued in accidents. The gnarly Scotsman came to New Zealand to run schools in advanced driving techniques at Manfeild Circuit near Palmerston North. Stewart told me that he won races because he treated the car well. He now advocates a driving style called Formula Finesse both on road and on track.

During the course that I was privileged to attend, one of the exercises was to lap Manfeild with a petfood bowl containing a loose ping-pong ball glued to the bonnet. The task was to achieve the lap in the fastest possible time without the ball coming out of the bowl. In other words, one had to drive smoothly. There were several similar tests of finesse. Almost all were won by a female motoring writer and long-time colleague of mine, Sandy Myhre, with whom Denny Hulme spent the last four years of his life.

Sandy was arguably our first female motoring writer, and initially experienced difficulties in getting executives of some car companies to take her seriously. The battle she fought and won made things much easier for the women who followed her, and it has been pleasing to see a number of women admitted to the New Zealand Motoring Writers Guild in recent years.

Another man of great vision was Auckland businessman Roly Crowther. Mr Crowther wanted to build a totally New Zealand designed car, and in 1971 he issued a prospectus to raise capital. He had built a prototype which I test drove at the Pukekohe race circuit, and the results of that test appeared in the prospectus, a copy of which I still have because it is an historic document. The prototype was powered by a German Wankel rotary engine but the intention was to buy engines from Subaru for the production line cars. The engine and transmission were to be the only components of the car that were not manufactured in New Zealand.

This was the first time I had experienced the Dutch-invented continuously variable transmission. Using a cone and belt in the gearbox, the gear ratios change not in defined stages as in an ordinary automatic gearbox, but in a smooth progression. It reminds one of accelerating in a speedboat. Although the little car went very well, unfortunately the investing public was not greatly interested. The money was not forthcoming and the all New Zealand car was stillborn.

Many years later Roly Crowther told me that with the benefit of hindsight, he felt the project would have been a financial disaster. But back then he was young and enthusiastic, two ingredients that can be found at the root of many an optimistic idea.

In the early 1970s, Henry Ford II visited New Zealand to turn the first sod for the building of a Ford plant in South Auckland. As a cadet reporter for the NZBC, I was invited to meet him. I could not believe what I was seeing in regard to the heavy brigade that surrounded him. I understood that under New Zealand law at that time it was illegal to carry a pistol. I can tell you that Mr Ford's entourage was somehow diplomatically immune. Their side arms stuck outboard of their garments as though they had been given a good feed of Bluff oysters. Mr

Ford was very charming and had all the time in the world for the kid from the TV station. We talked about how the Edsel car failed, how the Consul 315 failed, how the Corsair failed, and then I asked him about airbags. Yes, in the early '70s airbags were being experimented with. 'Peederr,' he drooled, 'airbags are for the birrrds. They are a fantasy.' Twenty-five years later they have become a standard fitment, and no-one would buy a new car that was without them.

Some time after Henry Ford's visit I was sent a book for review which was written by a Robert Lacey, an American. This book claimed that in the 1920s and '30s the Ford empire employed a strong-arm squad who went around the factory and the district physically ensuring that Ford interests were not being blocked or inhibited. In those times, the company also owned a Detroit newspaper that featured a certain amount of editorial that was anti-Semitic.

During Ford's visit, someone from Ford New Zealand pointed out a man in his entourage who was carrying a small leather case. This person tried to convince me that inside it was Mr Ford's favourite toilet paper. I thought that was nonsense — it was probably ammunition for all the side arms.

Let's Put This Car
to the Test

How long do they let you keep a test car for? Does your wife get to drive it? Do you have a special test route? Do you have a check sheet?

Motoring writers, I guess all writers, get asked all sorts of questions by their readers — these are just a few that are typical of what in today's parlance are called FAQs (Frequently Asked Questions).

The average period that I keep a car is about a week. Most companies feel that a week is about as long as they can spare a car, given that there are other journalists they want to offer it to as well, and given also that a car circulating the press corps is a car removed from the opportunity of a sale. Therefore it is not making them money, unless we all go into raptures about it in our publications and people buy that model by the zillion as a result.

Some writers, and I have been one, are approached to drive a car for a month or even several months, by way of what is called in the industry an extended road test. There is more than one reason why such an approach might be made. It may be that the distributors feel they know the writer well enough to be fairly certain that this particular model's qualities will greatly appeal to them. To leave the vehicle with the writer long term may result in their producing more than one story during the period of the test, thus increasing the amount of positive coverage gained for the vehicle.

In the case of a speciality motoring magazine, a car may be taken onto the office fleet with the express view of reporting to the readers regularly how the vehicle behaved over the period, what went wrong with it, what servicing it needed, and how each member of the staff adapted to the vehicle. British and American magazines will sometimes take a vehicle on for two years under such an arrangement.

When I have taken on a long-term test vehicle, I have continued with the usual weekly programme of test cars concurrently, trying to get time to drive both. Sometimes, test schedules and bookings become confused and total confusion reigns. My record is having eight test cars jammed into the driveway all at once. Since then I have managed to be a bit more organised, and have managed to keep it down to a dull roar.

Who is authorised to drive test cars has always been a matter of simple agreement between me and the distributors. Without exception, they have been and are happy for Anne to drive them. Firstly, they appreciate that a woman's view is important to me and that Anne will pick things that I may not. Secondly, she sometimes has to help me ferry cars to and fro. Some journalists who have the luxury of having staff photographers at their disposal send the photographer off in the car to find a nice background and take a picture, while the journalist gets on with other things. That, too, is acceptable to the distributors.

Letting your teenage offspring career around the place in a distributor's car is not acceptable, and understandably so, although it has happened. In one case I'm aware of, the car was crashed and the company became understandably testy with the journalist concerned.

If a speed camera ticket arrives at the offices of a distributor, it is sent on to the journalist who had the car on the day in question, and again, rightly so. Up to the time of writing, I have been sent one speed camera ticket by Holden, and another by Daihatsu. In the case of the Holden ticket, I pointed out to the police that their camera car was parked right on the change of speed limit from 100 km/hr down to 50 km/hr. I asked them how a driver could possibly be expected to make the transition in a matter of a few metres without risking a 200-car nose-to-tail accident. They agreed and cancelled the ticket. They later advised me that they had changed their operating procedures so that a speed camera car must be stationed at least 250 metres beyond the sign announcing a lower speed limit.

In the case of the Daihatsu, the Feroza model I was driving quite simply got caught up in a flow of traffic so that if I had tried to slow down I would have caused an accident. I told the police that I could prove it, suggesting they look up the three photographs snapped before mine and the three immediately after it. From this they would be able to establish the veracity of my assertion that I was in a moving block of traffic where it would be unsafe for me to try to slow down until it thinned out somewhat. They did as I suggested and agreed with me — that ticket was also cancelled.

These and other issues I have encountered along the way have proved to me that, by and large, if you have an honest and fair argument, the New Zealand police will listen. At the time of writing, I am yet to have a traffic conviction.

No, I have no special test circuit or route. A test car simply lives with me for the week, does what I do, goes where I want to go. After all, that is what everyone else's car does. This means some cars get to go long distances and on holiday, some don't. But as we live in Auckland's rural fringe, they all get a combination of town and country roads, and motorways. They all get to prove their abilities on hills and very twisty roads, too, because our home is high in the Waitakere Ranges west of Auckland. If I lived in suburbia, then I would certainly look at running my test cars over a special route that provided the variety of conditions necessary to assess them properly.

I used to carry a check sheet on a clipboard, but after all these years it is now lodged firmly on my cerebral cortex. I will share with you just a few of the categories I take note of; to record them all would take a couple of pages and would start to get boring. I look for assembly quality and finish; no excess of NVH (noise/vibration/ harshness); logical and easy placement of controls and instruments; all-round visibility for the driver; adequate comfort and room for front and rear passengers; imaginative styling both inside and out; safety features such as ABS (anti-lock braking systems), traction control and airbags; adequate acceleration; low degree of brake fade under constant breaking, such as during descent in a long, hilly stretch; acceptable fuel economy; ease of getting in and out; acceptable driving position; acceptable level of ride comfort; safe, stable and comfortable cornering; storage space for knick-knacks inside; acceptable boot or luggage space; a good heating/ ventilation system, and a very subjective one indeed . . . do I get pleasure from driving this vehicle?

All these questions and the many other categories on the list are judged, of course, against the price of the vehicle and the type of vehicle it is. I am not going to be nearly as harsh on a coupe when it comes to rear passenger leg room as I am on a large 6-cylinder sedan. And I am going to excuse the $14,000 Korean runabout for not having traction control for at least a year or two yet.

More often than not a test car will be handed over to a journalist clean and with a full tank of fuel. Any additional fuel one needs one buys oneself, or in the case of a lucky few, their publication buys it. There is no obligation to fill the vehicle again before returning it, although a few journalists do. The car will be fully insured, with the usual exclusions applying, drink-driving being foremost, as one would expect.

Do you write about every car? The answer in my case is almost every one. Very few do not get reviewed. But as my pages in the *National Business Review* are only published weekly, therefore fifty times a year, in the same week I will often review an important new model at length and a less important one briefly. How do I decide what is an important model and what is not for the purposes of this exercise? Well, the car that is a mere facelift or upgrade of an existing model is less important than a brand-new generation of cars.

Do you get blasé about them? The answer to that is yes. A certain creeping sameness has begun to engulf motor vehicles. When I began in this game, cars were screamingly different from one another. They went from the appalling to the barely accept-able. Many car makers and assemblers had much to be modest about back then. The Skoda S110, for instance, came with the promise that it had eight combinations of driver's seat position. It may well have had. What the publicity did not tell you was that you needed (1) an hour, and (2) a socket set to change anything.

Try to wash a Hillman Avenger and your hands became deeply lacerated and bled, so sharp were the bits of body trim on the car. Front-wheel-drive Austins and Morrises would chew through constant velocity (CV) joints in an alarmingly short time, with the result that they would click, clack and rattle along the road. To be fair, front-wheel-drive technology was reason-ably new then, although Citroën had been using it since the 1930s. And any Italian car was already rusting even though it was less than a year old — you could stand and watch, and take bets from people as to which part you would see daylight through next.

Today, so many cars are so good that finding differences and character is not easy. Italian cars are now excellent, and offer some of the best flair and style. The British lost most of their car industry, partly through arrogance and indifference to quality, and partly through trying to run it as a government department. I can recall visiting car factories in Britain during Maggie Thatcher's reign, and sullen workers would throw tools down heavily and scowl in resentment at the very idea of visitors being present. The Italians nearly lost their car industry for some of the same reasons as the British, but saved it just in time and turned it around.

What happens if a car company does not like what you have said about them or their product? The answer to that is anything from nothing at all to a one-year ban on being given information and offered test cars to drive.

General Motors New Zealand (now Holden New Zealand) banned me in about 1990 for a year. My sin was this. They were running a TV commercial that strongly suggested that a Korean-built Daewoo car they were distributing in New Zealand was in fact American. The ad featured ticker tape parades and all kinds of Americana. General Motors had even given the car the appellation Pontiac. All around the country old codgers who had owned and driven Pontiacs from the 1930s until the early '60s were becoming greatly excited and displaying behaviour problems at the bowling club and the RSA. And they were ordering these cars. At the same time, General Motors were running another ad for the Commodore. It had some ambitious bloke being invited to join the board of directors of some mythical company . . . something like Portaloo maybe. When he was asked what kind of car he would like to go with the job, our very assertive new business star would boom, 'I want a Commodore.' Well, I wrote a tongue-in-cheek column that paraphrased and merged the two ads. Jim was asked what sort of car he would like, and blurted, 'I want a Daewoo.' The chairman looked slightly nonplussed, and after a short pause replied: 'Oh. All right then. Just go down the corridor and it's the third door on the left.'

At this, General Motors' PR guy threw all his toys out of the cot. A complaint was laid with the Guild of Motoring Writers (which I had helped found) about my unprofessional behaviour, and General Motors struck me off its mailing and invitation lists for about a year, maybe a tad longer. Only a change in senior management at the company saw me invited back. Since then, the company has been blessed with successive managements that have been extraordinarily modern and enlightened, to the point that they dropped the Pontiac Le Mans from their range saying they were not happy with the car's quality. I hasten to add that Daewoo is now making world-quality products. Back then, they left a little to be desired.

The other company to ban me was Honda. If I recall correctly, and again this was in the early 1990s, they never exactly explained to me why they had taken this action. Suddenly, all the press information ceased to arrive, as did invitations to drive Hondas and to attend their functions. I think a combination of remarks or findings in my articles about Honda built up to breaking strain. Again, suddenly I was invited back and it was as though nothing had happened.

In both cases, other journalists kept me up with events and I went to friendly dealers to get drives of important cars, as I was concerned to keep my readers up with anything important regarding these brands. My publisher, Barry Colman, who owns the *National Business Review*, stood firmly behind me as he always has. When veiled suggestions were made that the paper should get a motoring writer who was more acceptable to the industry, Barry said that if one of his contributors was seriously out of line he would act; if, however, the contributor was simply being ingenuous, frank and honest, the complainants were wasting their time with him, despite the fact that, like any newspaper, *NBR* relied on advertising revenue.

Do distributors deliver the cars to you? On a few occasions, yes. But mostly, no.

Normally, a motoring writer must get himself or herself to a dealership or the distributor's office. This involves intricate arrangements for a second driver to drop one off for the pick-up, then pick one up after the drop-off.

It is not easy. But on some occasions car companies, sensing that one cannot always get that second driver, will offer to deliver a car.

In the UK it appears to be different. Several years ago I had an obsession about going back to England and showing Anne some of the places where I lived and went to school in Oxfordshire and Berkshire, before emigrating to New Zealand at the age of nine. My memories of these places were vivid, despite being so young when I left. Hearing of our plans, Rover volunteered to loan us a press car for this pilgrimage, given that exactly the same Rover cars were on sale in New Zealand and I could thus keep up with my road test schedule. On our arrival in the UK we stayed with friends in Wimbledon, and — can you believe this — one day there was a tap-tap-tap on the door of the apartment. A little man introduced himself as being from Rover, and asked if Sir would accept the keys for the car he had just parked outside the door. I thanked him and asked if he had transport back to wherever he had come from, for if not, I would drive him there.

'That's not necessary, Sir,' he said, oh so humbly. 'I have come down from Birmingham.' This man had driven from Rover in Birmingham to London, to deliver a press car to a journalist. British motoring writers tell me this is the norm there.

I simply could not bring myself to close the door on the little man from Rover, and tell myself that this is what the class system is all about. I know people who would have done that, and who would have delighted in telling the story for ever and a day. About how the little man from Rover drove all the way from Birmingham to London, found the right address at Wimbledon, handed over the keys to Sir, and how Sir snatched the keys, said 'Thank you, my good man,' thrust 50p at him, and shut the door. Perhaps it's living in New Zealand that has made me see things differently.

I demanded that he tell me how I could help him start his journey home. He said all he needed was to get to the nearest railway station; he had a special ticket that Rover purchased for their delivery drivers, and that would get him home. Since I was so insistent, perhaps I could run him to Wimbledon Station. No way would he accept tea, coffee or a snack at the apartment before setting out. And if, when we got back from our week-long drive in the counties, we were to leave the keys with the care-taker of the apartment block, he would return to Wimbledon and pick up the car after we had left for our flight back to New Zealand. I was led to wonder whether, in fact, the British are not their own worst enemies in the way that they doggedly adhere to the master/serf relationship in which their odious class system is rooted.

When we returned from our travels Anne and I did leave the keys with the caretaker, and hired a British phenomenon called a mini-cab to get us to the airport. It was diesel-powered, smelly, and rattly, and as far as I could tell it was an elderly Peugeot of some description.

We got onto the motorway, a serious London motorway. This was one evil, smelly car. I imagine the driver would have been able to concoct an evil sphincter-quiverer of a Vindaloo, but when it came to servicing and nurturing his vehicle, I sensed there were other things he would rather have been doing. The diesel engine got louder and louder and more and more rattly, and I began to feel quite glad it was not an underfloor engine of the type you get in some buses. If it had been, one of us would have been in great danger of getting a con rod right up our jacksie.

In the end something went bang very loudly, and the old Peugeot coasted to a halt on the shoulder — 30 kilometres away from the airport where we were due to check in 30 minutes hence. A flight home to New Zealand is not something that leaves every 35 minutes, and there were one or two arrange-ments with our offices at home and for Anne's small herd of turbo-charged cats that meant we would like to get home on time.

So we abandoned the hapless cabby in a sea of diesel oil and began walking along the shoulder of the motorway, towing some of the baggage on its own little wheels and humping the rest. My hope was to find a little town on the other side of the motorway barrier, where we would surely be able to hop over the grey steel Armco and get another cab. This was not to be.

Ten lanes away from us and travelling in the opposite direction, a white Range Rover with a Day-Glo stripe around its waist, blue flashing beacons on its roof, and emanating a klaxon-like sound pulled to a halt. Two policemen in anti-collision yellow jerkins leapt through the scarce gaps in the traffic and confronted us.

'What do you two think you are doing, walking along the motorway . . . Sir?'

I told them about the cab that had haemorrhaged a mile back. I showed them our air tickets and our New Zealand passports. I impressed upon them that we really needed to catch this flight, and as Kiwis we did not know that it was against the law to walk when the engine stopped.

Do you know, I am quite positive I saw a hint of a salute from one of these guys. Then they said they would get on the RT and call us another cab, which they did, and which arrived. The regrettable bit was that they were going to go back along the shoulder and 'do' the marooned Peugeot diesel cabby.

'Did he really let you out of the car on this incredibly dangerous motorway?' one of them demanded.

The fact was that he did, but only after a bit of insisting from me, and I worried about the fact that the poor bugger probably got charged with something, like looking at a policeman in a funny way.

As it turned out, when we got to the airport we were told we would have to go to Manchester — our aircraft had been redirected there because of fog. So we rode all night in a bus.

On climb-out from LA, our 747 ran into birds that were ingested into one engine. The engines prefer jet fuel. The crew had to shut down the engine, dump fuel over the sea and return to LAX. We were not meant to get home that week, I think. But eventually we did.

I mentioned earlier that logical placement of controls is one of the things I look for when I'm testing a car. It amazes me how the controls and switches in some vehicles are scattered all over the car, and that there is no standard system of placement. When you drive three different vehicles a week, at some stage you are sure to zap the wiper or washer when you want the indicator. The European Community likes its indicator switch on the left. Japan, which took its cues from the English cars that it shamelessly copied in the '50s, has stuck with the right where English cars once had it, but don't now. Britain has since gone the European way, which means the indicator stalk on the left. Korean cars have always had their indicators on the right because the Korean motor industry has modelled itself on the Japanese, with a view to grinding the Japanese industry into the dust one day. Which is slim thanks for the way the Japanese invested in the Korean industry in the late 1980s and taught it everything it knows.

Other controls migrate all over the place. I drove a Renault Megane for a week with the rear wiper going. The reason? I don't have time to read three manuals a week — each printed in nine languages, the first of which always seems to be Spanish — in order to locate an evasive switch or lever.

If the car's controls are not easy to locate and operate, I am not going to put my earning time into digesting yet another Concorde pilot's conversion textbook. Some car makers seem to think that the deeper and more complex the operation of their car is, and the more reading that is necessary to understand it all, the happier the customer will be that he has invested in a truly advanced technological package.

They may be right. A retired person spending $70,000, and with not a lot to do, may well lapse into delirium at the prospect of having to study a 250-page manual for a week. It makes him think he has got something hugely advanced. It fills in a week that would otherwise have been very boring. It diverts his attention from the perceived defects of his wife, which magnify one thousand-fold when he has nothing to do. It gives him something to talk about among neighbours and mates. And once he has learned where everything is and what everything does, he is truly in charge of his dotage.

I fully accept that one day I may well occupy that same turf. But right now, I cannot see why there is not a worldwide standard that says the window controls, light dipper and indicator stalk will always be in the same place. These are the controls that you need in the dark — they should be in the same place in every vehicle.

Have we not already been through all this pain with VHS and Beta? Did not Cessna give up making light single-engine planes for a decade because Americans, whose national sport is litigation, would sue the company every time a plane crashed?

'On the new model, they moved the throttle lever, Your Honour. As a result, my husband, Hyram B. Hyram Junior, sits before you in his wheelchair, completely oblivious to what is going on.'

It is a world in which we can all share the same computers, we can fax each other without difficulty, and work the Internet together. But cars will continue to have irritating (or maybe I should say characterful) differences for a good while yet.

OK, settle down folks and let's get this meeting started. I have called us together this morning because my department, Public and Customer Relations, needs some help. The sky seems to have fallen in again in regard to our range of fine vehicles. It falls to my department to try to put a positive spin on things. We haven't had quite such an uproar as this since the great cup-holder debacle of 1997. You will recall that episode. All the cup-holders in the cars had been made a millimetre too small in diameter, with the result that customers' cups were getting jammed in them. You will all recall that awful incident in Ooom-abladda, Australia. The customer wrenched hard to retrieve her cappuccino from the unyielding grip of the cup-holder, caused a fountain of scalding coffee, and the result was a 24-car pile-up. My department had to sort that one out, ladies and gentlemen. I am hoping to get the latest problem sorted out without quite as much negative publicity as we got last time, so I need your help.

There are two problems, actually. The first is that we are receiving a large number of complaints about the so-called tamper-proof speedos that we began fitting about five years ago. I see that John McVinyl is here today to represent the Department of Dashboards, Binnacles and Speedos. John, can you give us a rundown on just what the tamper-proof speedo is all about?

JOHN: Certainly. Upon reaching three to five years of age, every second one of our cars finds its way to New Zealand as a so-called used import. We became aware that somewhere along the line these cars were losing anywhere between 50,000 and 120,000 km from their odometers. People driving our cars were experiencing failures of all sorts of components. This was not good PR for us. The reason for the problems was that the cars had done three times the mileage the owners thought they had done. So in the mid-1990s we devised the tamper-proof speedo.

CLINT: I see, John. The problem, though, is that nearly 400 people have lost their fingers while working on these speedos. Even the Saudis have complained. They say they used to be the world leaders in the business of cruel and barbaric punishments, and they're upset at being eclipsed by a car company. This is causing great difficulties for my public relations department, John.

JOHN: That may be so, Clint. But if you contact New Zealand now, you will find that far fewer clocked cars are arriving there than ever before.

We have created a deterrent.

CLINT: Was it necessary, John, to include the audio chip? You know, the one that when the speedo is tampered with, says in a loud electronic voice 'Gotcha you devious little (racial reference) bastard. You may as well cancel the piano lessons.' These things make life very difficult for me, John. We have had faxes from Amnesty International and the Pope pleading for clemency for speedo flickers.

JOHN: Look, my department was asked to protect the good name of our 2-litre Fiasco GLX. I dispatched two people to New Zealand to look into the matter. They came back with ten crates of a dark beer called Speights and a device called a possum trap.

CLINT: What were the ten crates of dark beer for?

JOHN: For the departmental booze-up, if you must know, Clint. Speights just happens to be the best-tasting dark beer in the world. Apparently, if a New Zealand girl doesn't drink Speights and have huge hanungas, she has no marriage prospects there.

CLINT: And the trap thing?

John: This was an ingenious device used in New Zealand for trapping a breed of small animal that is slowly eating the entire country. We copied its mechanism for our tamper-proof speedo.

CLINT: We're going to have to change this mechanism from now on, John. I am going to suggest that you look for a way of linking it to the airbag system. Anyone tampering with the speedo gets the airbags in his face, along with the massive bill for replacing them. Let me know progress, would you? And try and make the message on the audio chip something a bit more acceptable.

Now the other item on the agenda is a problem that's been uncovered with the electric seat height adjuster on the Fiasco. Is there anyone here from Upholstery, Bolsters and Carpets? Ah, I see that Cush Ample is here to represent them. Cush, dear, have you seen the report on the electric seat height adjuster fatality in Texas?

CUSH: Not yet. Our email's got PMT. What happened?

CLINT: Well, it seems that this J.R. Ewing type, who was about six foot nine . . . around the neck . . . went to operate his power-operated seat height adjuster on the top-of-the range Fiasco. The problem appears to have been that the seat height adjuster did not stop operating when he let go of the button. The seat kept on rising. His head pushed the roof of the car up into a pyramid. Then the roof popped clean off the pillars. It was all a bit messy, Cush.

CUSH: Really? I recall that before you joined us, Clint, we had a similar problem with power-operated fore and aft seat adjusters. Someone got crushed to death against the steering wheel. The funeral director said she had the words SRS Airbag imprinted into her chest. But I don't recall a seat height adjuster problem before. I thought we had got the circuitry for the system sorted out long ago using crash dummies. Although it's true that during testing the odd crash dummy would end up with its head coming out of its bum.

CLINT: Cush, this kind of thing makes life very difficult for me. I want all owners contacted and told that for safety reasons we are going to establish their driving position, set the seat in the correct position, then unhook it from the car's electrics perman-ently. The chairman is irate. He says until we can get our act together, we can forget any idea of board approval to go ahead with our fantastic new sports car, the Orgasm. As you know, we have been on the verge of Orgasm for quite some time now and we have all been looking forward to it happening.

He is so irate that he is brandishing that ancient sword thing that he keeps in his office and has asked for two crash dummies to be sent up. I suggest, Cush, that we don't send him two crash dummies with their heads hanging out of their bums. All right. Let's get back to work.

May I See Your Licence, Please?

On 14 June 1964, at Massey, West Auckland, a travesty took place. Peter Noel Gill, a secondary school pupil, passed the test for the New Zealand driver's licence. He was delighted at the time and danced little pirouettes when he got home. But in retrospect, I and half my fifth form class breezed through the driver's licence test.

At that time, the tests were conducted by what were called traffic officers. They were a separate body from the police, and they enforced traffic law on the nation's roads. In preparation for my test, my father made sure his 1954 Hillman Minx had a current warrant of fitness — it would be less than helpful if the officer riding with me were to notice that the vehicle did not have its safety sticker. I cleaned and polished the car. We arrived several minutes early for the test, so as not to keep the officer waiting. The kindly officer asked me to read off an eye-test chart, then popped a few questions from the Road Code about traffic laws. Then he climbed into the front passenger's seat of the old

67

green Hillman, and directed me to drive a mile on what was then a rural main road. I did that. Then he asked me to do a three-point turn. I did that. Then he found a slope and had me do a hill start. I did that. Then he said, 'That'll do. Take me back to the office.' At the office, he invited me in for a cup of tea while he wrote out the chit to say that I had passed. And that was it.

Adding to the travesty of 14 June 1964, at Massey, West Auckland, was the fact that I did not merely receive a licence to drive a car. Another category was automatically granted, that of the so-called 'power cycle or moped'. Any New Zealander who passed the licence test for a car was automatically presumed to be competent to ride a motorcycle of up to 50 cc in engine power, regardless of whether they had ever ridden one in their life.

This seemed a harmless enough idea, given the low power of such machines. Except, that is, for what happened some years later. A law change abolished the moped category. From then on, a full motorcycle licence would be required of anyone wishing to ride a two-wheel powered machine. However, anyone who wished to continue riding his or her moped, for which they had been granted a licence along with the car licence, could apply to the authorities to have his or her licence extended to include the new motorcycle category without being required to take a test. From that day on, both Anne and I have held full motorcycle licences. If we decide to have a midlife crisis and go out and buy ourselves a Harley, any law enforcement officer checking our licences will see that they include the motorcycle category and therefore appear legal.

Even if we were weaving along on our new Harley having trouble controlling it, he would be unlikely to suspect that we hadn't earned our licence. He would probably think that these people had just stepped up from a sophisticated bike and were still in the throes of trying to tame the Hog.

Hundreds of thousands of New Zealanders driving today got their licences in just such a way. One of the problems with writing a book of this nature is that things sometimes change, and in the short time between my writing these words and you showing appallingly bad taste by choosing to read them, things may be different. But as I write, it is my understanding that the next time I will be legally required to demonstrate my driving ability to a testing officer will be at the age of 74. Therefore, people who got their licences in their teens, and pretty damned easily too, need not concern themselves about having to prove their on-road skills until the age of 74, the way New Zealand law stands as I write. This situation has existed for decades.

In the early 1990s, a driver's licence was not that much harder to get than it was in 1964. I know this because in 1992, while a co-presenter on the TV series 'Wheels', I took the test to illustrate a story we were filming about driver's licence testing. I was also the presenter of an educational video called 'Passing the Test' which is sold in bookshops. The on-road test is more comprehensive now. But the theory is a sort of scratch and win affair with multiple-choice answers, the level of difficulty of which would be a challenge only to a three-year-old.

I have bored you with the fact that I hold a private pilot's licence, which I obtained in 1997. This was an extraordinarily difficult qualification to achieve. I appreciate that things are always going to be hard if you are an imbecile. But in order to fly a private single-engined piston plane in daylight hours with passengers, I had to sit hours and hours of theory examinations following a long course of lectures and study, complete a comprehensive syllabus in the air which took many, many hours, and take a comprehensive medical examination. More to the point, every two years I must prove my skills to a qualified instructor. If the instructor is unhappy about any aspect of my abilities, I will be required to retrain in that aspect. And the medical is every two years. When you reach 50 it is annual. The authorities are thus able to ensure I can see and hear properly and that my blood pressure is acceptable for a person in charge of a lethal machine.

I am not proposing that anything quite so draconian should attach to the driver's licence. What I am saying, though, is that hundreds of thousands of Kiwis were virtually given the licence on a platter and have never had to worry about maintaining their level of skills since.

A visit to Australia, the US or Britain will quickly and amply demonstrate that the level of New Zealanders' driving skills is unfortunately not high. It is only a matter of two generations ago that we were essentially a rural society. There was relatively little traffic on our roads. Rural people almost had the road to themselves, and did not have to develop attitudes that took account of the needs and safety of other road users. Things were fairly casual in the suburbs too. These people taught the next generation to drive, passing on some attitude problems that are less than appropriate in today's burgeoning New Zealand towns and cities. Attitude has never been part of the syllabus for the New Zealand driver's licence. It is not speed or alcohol that is the major killer on New Zealand roads — it is poor attitude.

A good attitude would take care of the speed and alcohol problems. But it would also see people letting others into gaps in lines of traffic. It would see people maintaining lane discipline on motorways instead of weaving through the traffic, lurching across every lane as a gap presents itself. Attitude would bring the tailgater to his or her senses. Tailgating is endemic in New Zealand.

Drive in Europe, the US or Australia and watch how people keep their distance at cruising speed. Watch, too, how they choose their lane on the motorway and stay in it. That is because people drive at a uniformly sensible speed. They choose the lane that is moving at the speed that best suits them, and they stay there.

In terms of traffic education, the authorities in New Zealand have spent up large on TV commercials that depict horrific accidents. In these commercials, speed or alcohol is always blamed. Nowhere, at no time, do we see little commercials that show people doing polite, helpful and sensible things on the road, with a message that says, 'What Mary did there wasn't a bad idea, was it? She let that van into a gap. She and the van driver feel quite good about that. It's all part of helping your fellow Kiwi.'

Neither do we see little vignettes that reinforce our knowledge of the road rules. Can you imagine how often most New Zealanders would have looked at a road code since getting their licence?

Now, before you start to think that I am getting all lofty and superior and beginning to preach at you, let me make the point that the Kiwi driver is asked to cope with some impossibly difficult roads.

Take New Zealand's busiest stretch of road, the southern motorway section of State Highway 1 in Auckland. In at least two places, a major on-ramp is followed immediately by an off-ramp. So we have vehicles trying to force themselves on to the motorway at the same time as others are trying to forge their way through them to get off. Others still, simply want to carry on straight ahead. This is an appalling situation and one in which the designers have much to answer for. The same motorway has off-ramps exiting to both the left and the right in close proximity to each other.

Many of our roads are twistier and coarser of surface than in the rest of the western world. There are reasons for this — the hilly nature of much of New Zealand, the lack of population to finance better roads, and the fact that we use coarse river gravel bonded to tarmac for many of our road surfaces. We use the gravel instead of smoother compounds because it is cheap and there is an abundance of it. Over the years this gravel has caused problems with high noise levels from tyres, and many a distributor has been forced to experiment with different types of tyre in order to reduce the cochlea-splitting roar from tyres fitted to cars in countries where the roads have smooth surfaces.

Assistant Commissioner Phil Wright, for many years New

Zealand's most senior traffic policeman, once made a salient comment about this. He said that the New Zealand roading system was 'third world'. Despite the many great feats of engineering whereby we have roads built through extremely difficult terrain such as Arthur's Pass and the Gentle Annie, I agree with him. Our roads are narrow, and tend to have sharper bends than those in other developed countries. There are not many kilometres of motorway, and almost none outside the main cities.

The reason I was in conversation with Mr Wright was because I had some difficulty accepting the way speed cameras were operated shortly after their introduction. I mentioned earlier the way the camera cars would sit right on the spot where the speed limit changed from 100 km/hr to 50 km/hr. To his credit, Mr Wright listened and changed some of the operating procedures for speed camera cars.

He told me the reason they were introduced was to try to get traffic flowing at more uniform speeds. If those who travel at very high speeds are taken out of the equation, those who are left in any traffic stream are travelling at a less diverse range of speeds. A stream of traffic in which every vehicle is being driven at approximately the same speed is a safer stream of traffic to be in. It is when speedsters begin to duck and dive among the slower vehicles that accidents happen.

While I could appreciate this point, I kept getting letters from ordinary responsible New Zealanders who were simply off to bowls or the RSA in their Hyundais when zap — in a flash of orange light they were $100 the poorer. For a time people became frustrated by this. There was even one incident where an enraged man approached the speed camera car with an axe and began to smash the camera unit. Partly because people have become used to the cameras and thus more aware of speed limits, and partly because the police have tuned the cameras to offer a reasonable margin for driver error, the number of complaints I receive from my readers has reduced to a dull roar.

About that midlife crisis and the bike: I have been thinking about a bike for some years, since well before I qualified for anything associated with mid-life. I cannot put my finger on what it is that is so aphrodisiac about the idea. I have certainly noticed that a number of pilots in my aero club seem to also enjoy bikes, and I wonder if there is any commonality between the two experiences.

A long time ago I had a battleship-grey Puch moped that I found in the shed of a flat I rented as a student. It had long been abandoned by someone, but I breathed life into it and it ran well enough. I used it mostly for riding into the middle of the lounge room at parties, which seemed a pretty cool thing to do in 1968. But my serious transport was always a car.

To my surprise, when I recently mentioned to Anne the possibility of acquiring a bike she was not at all averse to the idea; she has more experience with them than I do, even if only on the Honda 50 she rode as a teenager. A colleague of mine, Paul Owen, is an experienced motorcyclist. I suggested to Paul that I felt it was not only optimistic but positively dangerous for us to go out and buy a bike and expect to be competent and safe with so little experience. He agreed, and promised that if and when we do go looking for a bike he will advise us about what motorcycle riding courses are available. He also said he would advise us on the best machine to buy so that we could get our motorcycling skills up to scratch without the worry of having to control an impossibly heavy and powerful machine. Later, we will graduate from that training bra machine, but probably not to a Harley.

When I was in California recently, where I always seem to see more Harleys per square centimetre than almost anywhere else in the world, a non-believer quipped: 'What do a Harley and a Rottweiler have in common? They both love going out on Sunday morning with Dad, and then coming home just before dusk on the back of some extremely kind person's ute.'

* * *

73

It is Friday night at Albany, just north of Auckland on that aortic artery, State Highway 1. Ahead of me in the uncharitable darkness I make out the balletic dance of reflective jackets. It's a police road block, checking principally for drivers who have had a tipple. I haven't. But these luminescent officers of the law, waving their torches as a conductor does a baton, will soon think that I have had a mega tipple. For when I get to the head of the queue of drivers who are variously wetting their pants, looking for a chance to do a quick U-turn, dosing themselves desperately with breath freshener, and recording their court defence into their dictaphones, I go to wind down the driver's window so that the waiting officer can do his or her thing.

There's the officer at the driver's window of my Jeep Cherokee test vehicle now, with regulation-issue Eveready Skull Cracker torch and alcohol sniffer. I hit the button. Down goes the left rear window. I hit another. Down goes the left front window. The officer's face has gone from latex to cement. I try again. Now I do not expect you to believe this, so don't if you would rather not. But down goes the right rear window. The officer's face goes from cement to granite. Finally, I get the correct button, but not without producing a shot of windscreen cleaner water right over the roof of the car as I do so. The officer is convinced he has got a kill. In comes the alcohol sniffer device and I am told to keep my hands away from all buttons. Rightly, he is concerned that he could lose an arm. I am asked to state my name and address. This gives the sniffer enough exhaled air to detect whether I have been drinking or not. He cannot believe that the machine is giving him a resounding negative result. He turns it upside down and shakes it.

A sense of fairness to my fellow Kiwi ignites a need in me to explain. He is a fellow citizen, doing his job, and doing a job that by and large needs doing, even if from time to time I disagree with some of the methodology and thinking employed by the constabulary. I explain that I drive three or four different cars a week as part of what I do. I explain to him what it is, in fact, that I do, and how I picked up this vehicle a mere 40 minutes earlier, and how he would not believe the disparity in where controls are placed and how they are laid out from vehicle to vehicle, maker to maker.

He needs an excuse to defuse, and accepts my speech with something approaching fawning deference. He wishes me a very good evening, comes amazingly close to touching the peak of his cap, stands back, and waves me on.

The same thing has happened to Anne. Stopped routinely by the police one night because she had forgotten to turn her lights on in a brightly lit city street, she had trouble finding the correct power window button. Coincidentally, she too was driving a Jeep Cherokee test vehicle that she had never driven before in her life. For some reason, a standard police-type question is, 'Who owns this vehicle?' Knowing only that some kind of import agency represented Jeep, and unlike me having no direct contact with them, she had no choice but to say: 'I have no idea, Officer. It was the easiest one to get out of our driveway.'

After some further explanation the officer took a few notes and let her go. That was the end of the matter. I know it is fashionable to crucify the police. I have been out with them on patrol on a number of occasions as part of my TV or writing work. I can honestly say that if you had an understanding of the job from the standpoint of the person trying to do it, you might be more balanced in your criticism.

This is hard stuff to retell. But I have witnessed Maori folk whose eyes flashed angrily as they hopped with warlike demeanour from one foot to the other while berating the officer who had stopped them for an alleged misdemeanour. They berated him on the grounds that in their view this country belonged to the Maori, so therefore Auckland's southern motorway belonged to Maori. So therefore the officer had no legal right to stop and remonstrate with a Maori driver. The Maori driver was not subject to Pakeha law and could do what he liked.

I have witnessed young women stopped by a male officer employing every technique available to them to get off a speeding ticket. If feigned charm and false allure did not work, some would swiftly change tack and talk about the urgent onset of a period, evidence of which they were prepared to show the male officer if necessary.

One poor guy who was stopped by the officer I was riding with had the simplest excuse I ever heard during my times going out on patrol. He was not lying. He was genuine. His plea? His marriage was in rigor mortis, his wife did not share any of his interests in life nor his bed, he was seeing another woman, and to have to explain to his wife why he had received a ticket for being in a certain place at a certain time was something he had planned on doing next year, not next month. To be fair to the officer I was riding with, blokey excuses like that one, genuine though it was, did not wash any better than those about sudden menstruation, or the Treaty of Waitangi.

The traffic police are certainly protective of anyone from any emergency service who is in uniform. When I was a volunteer firefighter, my brigade was attending an incident one night in which a power pole had been knocked over and there were high-tension lines draped across a main road. In full night-glow reflective uniform, I was flagging down and redirecting traffic into a side road and around the danger. A traffic policeman arrived to give us a hand. He sat in his car to send a situation report over the radio to his base before getting out to help. As he did so, he saw some idiot driver who was unwilling to have his journey interrupted try to run me over. I have never seen a dressing down like the one that driver got from that officer. And after he had done that, he came over to make sure I was OK.

Again, I know my stance is probably not a popular one. But it is my view, and always has been, that the New Zealand traffic police and their predecessors the Ministry of Transport were and are a pretty reasonable bunch. In all these years I have only had to take up the issue of over-zealousness or brainlessness on the part of an individual officer on three occasions. On general departmental policy and operational procedure, I guess I would have taken up the cudgels on a further twenty to thirty occasions. That averages out to once a year. To take up such issues is part of my job, after all. I have only taken such action when I have been extremely sure of my case, or that of the upset reader, listener or viewer who has contacted me. I say quite humbly that on each occasion I received either an apology or a reasonable explanation, and often both.

I have always enjoyed an open invitation to visit the New Zealand traffic police, ask questions, receive answers, and ride with the officers. The fair operation of speed cameras, which I have mentioned earlier, was probably the biggest and most important of the issues I have taken up and had success on. The second most important coup was the issue of stopping traffic on major routes at 10 a.m. on business days to check for alcohol, warrants of fitness, registration and Uncle Tom Cobley-and-all. This was popular with the New Zealand Police in 1996 and 1997. Stopping New Zealanders going about their lawful business at ten in the morning and creating queues kilometres long, causing missed appointments and undelivered cargoes, is something that got well and truly up my snorer.

At one road block on a major Auckland arterial road, I counted twenty officers on the job. That same month there had been national headlines that said urgent 111 calls were not being answered because of lack of personnel. My mailbox confirmed my concerns. I protested loudly, in national columns and by direct communication with the police. In my view, citizens have the right to go about their daily business without being detained, unless they have been observed breaking the law or are under reasonable suspicion.

With twenty other drivers I had plenty of time to think about this issue as I sat in a queue of traffic being processed by police one weekday morning on Auckland's North Shore. Just as I inched up to the front after a twenty-minute delay, rehearsing my demand to be presented to the officer in charge of this operation, they seemed to get the idea that they had become Public Enemy Number One, quickly took down the barriers, scooped up the cones, and waved us all on to our now hour-late day. Have you heard the term coitus interruptus? Well for me, being two cars away from remonstrating with the officer in charge felt just like that.

Lately the traffic police have begun to listen to what the people are saying. In part at least, they now take the arguments of Middle New Zealand on board. At the time of writing they have changed a number of operating procedures. For some time now they have been operating small road blocks with the emphasis on moving people through very quickly and not allowing queues to form. This is wise, as they are paid by our taxes, must shop where we do, and must send their kids to the schools we send ours to. All those things are made easier for them when they take a fair and reasonable approach to their jobs, which most do.

Over the years I have found it most instructive, comforting too, to observe that Kiwis have an innate sense of fairness. You see it in queues, in bars, in courts, schools, and on juries. It is everywhere. Officious law enforcement officers who do not play by this rule find eventually that they and their families have a very hard row to hoe in New Zealand society.

DETOUR

'Mate, I tell you it's true. Five minutes ago I saw a kangaroo run across the road wearing a 4X beer T-shirt.'

'Don't come the raw prawn with me, mate. Perhaps you had too much 4X yourself last night at the Holden media reception.'

'I'm telling you there's a damned great red roo leaping around out there with a 4X T-shirt on!'

The mate I refer to is old E.J. Waggin of Oomabladda, long-time motoring columnist for several Australian papers. Actually, E.J. is not the sort to have you on. What was even more convincing was that his co-driver, a serious Tasmanian fellow wearing shorts and leather jandals, was agreeing with him. We were filling up our convoy of test cars somewhere in the middle of Western Australia, at a one-pump gas station with a noisy and labouring bowser that had clock hands on it. The bowser visibly shook as it gurgled away, trying to slake the thirst of thirteen Commodores that had swept in like a desert whirlwind. E.J. took out his trusty old Nikon camera, loaded a new roll of film, spat on the film 'to stop it jamming, ya know', and sellotaped the back of the filthy old photographic instrument closed.

'I'm going back,' he declared in a voice reminiscent of an old McCulloch chainsaw. He gathered up the fibrous Tasmanian and roared off in the direction of his last sighting of the shirted marsupial. The rest of us had only had enough time to down a Pepsi each when E.J. returned in a dust cloud to rejoin his fellow motoring writers.

'Got the bugger,' he declared, waving the filthy old Nikon in the air in a victory gesture. Back in Perth, he headed directly for the photolab of one of the city's newspapers. And sure enough, the images clearly showed a large kangaroo wearing a 4X beer T-shirt.

The photo appeared in several major newspapers.

A few days later a football team from a small Western

Australian town settled the mystery. Their bus had hit the animal. Being tired and emotional, the footballers had piled out of the bus to remove the body from the road. They decided to hold a form of funeral service in its honour, which involved each team member sinking a couple of tinnies and the dressing of the animal in a T-shirt that had been stinking the bus out for some reason.

They had no sooner got the shirt onto the animal than it got up, leered at them and loped off.

A Wheel in Each Corner and Some Help from Peter Sellers

'Yes, Peter. It can be done in a Mini.'

The female voice which carried so much assurance was that of my old TV News friend Marion Hazen, who had moved on to become deputy editor of the glossy magazine *Style*.

Marion had asked me what I would be writing about for her next issue. It was 1998, and I had just been invited to drive the latest Mini. Yes, it was still being built and sold new in New Zealand in 1998. In small numbers, of course.

I saw my first Mini at the 1961 Kumeu Show, one of those agricultural and pastoral shows that New Zealand is famous for. These shows are a moving pastiche of highly energetic sheepdogs, impossibly oversized pumpkins, rows and rows of preserved fruits that the judge has to pick winners from without ever tasting them, black-singleted men chopping down posts for prizes, and the always-present smell of hot dogs and tomato sauce.

I challenge any reader to turn away from that particular odour. It is part of the birthright of a man to savour, celebrate and then give in to it. I have noticed that many a woman shares this particular gene. That special odour, the odour of hot dog and tomato sauce, weakens a person, breaks them down. It has them homing in on its source (and sauce) like a heat-seeking missile. Whatever high-flown diet a person may be on (and I have never been on one because I don't believe in them), the odour of hot dogs and tomato sauce will thoroughly sabotage it and destroy their belief system.

Anyway, it was in such an environment that I first saw the Mini. I was a kid, a member of the Whenuapai Air Scouts. We were taken on as messengers by the show's organisers, cellphones a day or two away from being invented. And here, in a roped-off enclosure, was the car that had hijacked the attention of half the world. Sir Alec Issigonis had brought us the sturdy Morris Minor. Now, he had excelled himself. For here was a car that pushed the boundaries of every automotive value we had ever known. A wheel in each corner. Engine placed east-west, across the car. Gearbox and sump combined to save space. Front wheel drive. Not the world's first, but front wheel drive was far from the norm in 1959 when the Mini was unleashed in the UK. So front wheel drive just added to the car's quirkiness.

It was a car that, in my humble view, progressed the whole of cardom. Car designers and manufacturers needed someone to tell them that the war had been over for about fourteen years. For the British, it was time to move on from stately and funereal-looking canal-barge-like cars with heavy bodies and mournful lines that almost wreaked of formaldehyde. It was time to break out. Issigonis did that. He created a car that used space like no other had ever done before. The tight packaging of the engine and gearbox due to the transverse mounting of the tiny power plant that held onto its gearbox and sump like someone holding their elastically failed pants up in a very small cubicle . . . this formula led to a whole new cult in cars. And in everything else really. Mini-skirts immediately followed, as British culture followed Sir Alec into a new break-out, celebratory, youthful phase. The Mini culture came and went, came again, and went. Such are the dynamics of fashion. Whether the Mini culture is here or temporarily absent, I would like to make this observation: the woman I will look at all night will be the one with the brain, and the long graceful skirt. With the thigh-high split in it. And the hose with the glimmering Lycra in it. If you know what I mean.

I digress. I was speaking of Sir Alec and the first Mini. It is said that when the first Mini was driven out of the factory, it stopped due to the rain. But as the years went by, I and my fellow students and then young workers revelled in the athletic delights of the Mini, and its spin-off, the four-door 1100. To be fair, no car that I had driven before the 1100 steered so laser-accurately, and handled so well. No car before it made use of space so well. No car seemed to have such an enthusiastic burst of power. These cars were fresh air to us, even though when they first arrived they were hard for us younger ones to afford.

Of course there was a price to pay for all this wonderful innovation. Minis and 1100s hated wet weather. And they suffered from weak CV joints, which I will explain in a minute. And some models also sagged badly suspension-wise.

A CV or constant velocity joint is a complex unit that transmits drive in a front-wheel-drive car. It allows a wheel to be both driven and steered at the same time. This means that the wheel can be in any plane, due to steering needs, and will still receive drive power. Pretty damned complex really. Even so, in those early Mini/1100/1300/1800 days, they were fairly short-lived. The problem was first signalled by a clattering noise. Within three weeks of that happening, your CV joints would be so badly worn that the car would be immobilised.

I mentioned that Minis didn't like the rain. The Mini owner's best friend was a can of CRC, that magical compound that instantly dried ignition parts. Still does. Whenever you went out in the rain, you took your can of CRC. The distributors on some of these cars were right behind the radiator grille. My wife Anne, who for years took breakdown calls at the AA and dispatched help, sent hundreds of patrolmen to cars with so-called wet ignition, usually meaning Minis and 1100s and their relatives. In so many cases, rain had blown through the grille onto the electrics.

Anyway, I began this chapter by speaking of Marion, my excellent and characterful TV News mate turned glossy mag deputy-editor. 'So your next column for *Style* is going to be about the Mini, is it it?' quizzed the rambunctious Marion.

'Yes, it is. They are still making them in 1998. And I have just test driven one.'

'Christ,' she responded. 'They are still making the old Mini in 1998. Well let me tell you, it can be done in a Mini. It has been done in a Mini. The only problem is that you have to tilt the seats forward. They have a nasty habit of falling back down again and hitting you on the back of the ankles.'

'Thanks, Marion. Not that I am really interested these days.'

The qualities of the Mini were not well recognised by the buying public at first. Initial sales were slow. The cars were the butt of cartoonists' jokes. It was not until the likes of Lord Snowdon, Princess Margaret, Twiggy, Lulu, Spike Milligan, Peter Sellers and other celebrities of the day began buying them and being seen in them that public sales took off.

The Mini raised car design from the dead. The very dead. The Mini and the 1100 were not perfect, but despite their need to have new CV joints yearly and to have the suspension gas-pumped up, they were cars that made a difference. They told the world that front wheel drive was here to stay. They told the world, too, that cars now had sharp acceleration and precise steering. No car before had offered such accurate control.

The Mini and the 1100 were major staging points in the history of the car.

Meanwhile, the much less depressed Americans were

concentrating on excess and fantasy. Their stylists and marketers had decided that rocketry and jet fighter aircraft represented the ultimate in power and excitement, and set forth to make cars ape them. So we saw the fins, the Boeing type dashboards, the tail lights that looked like firework displays and the bulbous bumper overriders that had the British accusing them of being taken off breast-feeding too early.

Some of these cars got to Australia and New Zealand, but because they were originally designed to be left hand drive they were not as readily available as British cars.

And none contributed to the sum total of knowledge and wisdom in the auto industry to the degree that the Mini did. Front wheel drive/transverse engine became almost the industry norm for small cars and for some medium-sized ones too. It remains a popular format today.

DETOUR

OK, ladies and gentlemen. Thanks for attending this meeting today. It's been called for the purpose of acquainting you with our next major vehicle project.

This is the first time we have met since I had the pleasure of announcing board approval of our new sports car project, the Orgasm and its all-wheel-drive variant, the Orgasm Multiple.

Now, I'm sure you have all heard the phrase 'If it looks like a duck, walks like a duck and quacks like a duck, then it's probably a duck.' This has been sound wisdom for decades. However, in the tradition of this, the most innovative vehicle manufacturing company in the world, we are about to completely disprove that theory. This project is to be called Project Dingbat.

After considerable research, our marketing department is quite convinced that there is a market for a vehicle that looks like a four-wheel-drive, complete with squared-off chunky guards, 16-inch open slatted wheels, spare wheel slapped firmly on the rear door, and riding higher off the road than, for instance, our current 2-litre Fiasco XLE sedan. Note very well what I said just then, ladies and gentlemen. I said, 'looks like a four-wheel-drive'. But in fact, you will be able to buy it with the option of two-wheel-drive only, for a price 25 per cent lower than the four-wheel-drive version. The two-wheel-drive will be known to us and to the dealer chain as the 'Impostor'. But that term is not to be mentioned within the hearing of the customer. The two versions will have identical badging. So, any Dingbat you see might be a four-wheel-drive or a two-wheel-drive. (The author later learned several vehicle manufacturers had taken his advice. You can now buy grunty 4WD's with stunningly brilliant rear-wheel-drive only, and for very good prices.)

We fully admit that this a brave move. The only precedent for it that we could find anywhere in the world dates back to the very late 1960s and early 1970s, in a small settlement off the east coast of Australia known as New Zealand. In that country, the small aboriginal car industry that existed there at the time took a Skoda Octavia chassis, engine and gearbox and built a vehicle onto it which they called the Trekka. The Trekka looked for all the world like a Land Rover, except that it was painted in very lively colours. But it had two-wheel-drive only. There never was a four-wheel-drive version, nor was there ever intended to be, such was the perverse humour of the people who lived in this settlement at the time.

People used to take these Trekka things into all kinds of impossible situations, and apparently, time after time, you could see Trekkas being pulled out of bogs by farm tractors. Things have changed in the two and a half decades that have passed since those times. Our research suggests that only ten per cent of the four-wheel-drive vehicles produced in the world ever go off-road, excluding those produced for the military.

Recently we sent a couple of our researchers to New Zealand to see if they could find any owners or former owners of the remarkable Trekka. But it seems that the owners and every last trace of the vehicles themselves have completely disappeared. Some lines of inquiry suggested that the owners drowned in their stranded vehicles in bogs, marshes and riverbeds. Other lines of inquiry suggest that Trekka ownership is something nobody talks about or admits to in those dark and shaky isles. It reminds one of that joke, doesn't it? You know the one.

What's the difference between a Lada and a sheep? Not a lot. You wouldn't want to be seen getting into the back of a sheep, either, would you?

But on a more seemly note, ladies and gentlemen, our trip to New Zealand to learn more about the phenomenon of a vehicle that looks like a four-wheel-drive but isn't was a complete waste of time really.

We understand that the Trekka thing did have one benefit for New Zealand, however. It spawned the idea for a new form of recreational sport known as whitewater rafting. The country had just given its kiwifruit technology away on a platter to the rest of the world, so it needed something to replace that export revenue, preferably something that you didn't have to plant, grow, nurture, pack and freight. Such as a raging river. We hear someone got stranded fording a river in his Trekka and bounced 70 miles downstream from the mountains to the sea in the vehicle. On the way he worked out that the ride would be more comfortable if he substituted a rubber raft for a Trekka, and a new sport was born. Anyway, I digress.

Optional extras on our two-wheel-drive Dingbat will be a dummy high/low ratio transfer case lever next to the gear lever, dummy exhaust snorkel kit, and life-like plastic replica of an electric winch that can be mounted in conjunction with a life-like plastic replica of a bull bar on the front bumper. Our merchandising department will feature a wide range of fashion accessory products that will support this vehicle. Chief among these will be a new product called 'The Brown Stuff'. This is our line of authorised spray-on mud. The cans will have no CFC in their propellant. Instead, the aerosol effect will be derived from expanding methane, gathered in the process of dredging only the world's finest swamps and marshes to gather 'The Brown Stuff'. Our mechanising department will also offer the official Dingbat baseball cap. This will be available with the peak sewn on to the back or the front, as required. The logo on it will carry the line, 'I'm a proud Dingbat owner and I know something that you don't.'

And finally, ladies and gentlemen, in the Dingbat and Dingbat Impostor we have decided to go for the world record in the numbers of cup-holders provided in any vehicles less than four metres in length. The record is currently held by the Chrysler Grand Cherokee and Volkswagen Sharan. I am not sure why Volkswagen chose a tarty girl's name for the world's most refined people carrier. But then, hey folks, they fought BMW in the street to get ownership of Rolls-Royce just to get the name, and got everything but the name. Now they're stuck with a bunch of barge-like cars hammered together by sullen and resentful Poms while BMW runs away with the real prize, the name plate.

Anyway, the number of cup-holders we are shooting for, ladies and gentlemen, is . . . wait for it . . . 37!

OK. That's it, thanks. Crash testing begins tomorrow morning at dawn.

9

Excuse Me, But What's the Best Car You've Ever Driven?

Towards the end of 1998 there came one magnificent week in which I test drove Audi's flagship, the V8-powered S8, a Porsche Boxster, an Alfa Romeo 156, and Volvo's then-new flyer of a coupe, the C5 turbo. I had them all for several days, all for the same several days.

There are times when you really have to force yourself to appreciate a car objectively, and to give equal time, attention and mileage to all comers.

I am often asked the question 'What is the best car around?' Or 'What is the best car you've driven?' All motoring writers endure this. It is an unwritten rule among us that we are always very polite and as helpful as possible in such circumstances. After all, we are in an extremely privileged position and it would be to our detriment if any of us lost sight of that fact. Many of those who ask us such questions are our readers. Within the bounds of reason, we owe them the time of day when they approach us personally, for without readers our publications would not exist. We would be out of a job.

Even so, it is usually necessary to ask the questioner to provide a little more focus. Best car in a specified price range? Best car for a family of five? Best car for a single woman? Best sports car? Best sedan? Best car capable of towing an eight-metre fibreglass hoon-boat with twin 250 horsepower Mercury outboards? Best lifestyle vehicle or four-wheel-drive? Best car for fuel economy? Or best car for simply offering a hedonistic, utterly visceral 'wow' experience?

Like wine, food and lovers, these things will ever be subjective. But because this type of question is asked so often, I am happy to stick my ever-thickening neck out and list a few cars that have stood out in some way.

Taking the decade of the 1990s and looking at cars that were simply awesome to behold and drive, the Honda NSX genuinely deserves a very high place in this ranking. You may be surprised that I have cited this Japanese car ahead of a Ferrari, Maserati, Lamborghini or Porsche. Fact is, the NSX does all that any of them do but does it in a most user-friendly way. Despite that stunning Formula One-bred performance, that balance, that poise, that timeless silhouette, this is a car that's easy to get in and drive.

This car's handling personifies Honda's immersion in Formula One. To look at, it is evocative of a Le Mans racer. It is an exquisite balance of poise and grace. It is a coupe, although there was a removable hardtop version as well. The NSX has a mid-mounted 3-litre V6 transversely situated engine that growls like a famished tiger. Here I defer to one of the best automotive wordsmiths I know to help me make my point. L.J.K. Setright, writing an introduction to a book commissioned by Honda to help introduce the NSX, put it this way:

Honda have disdained the juvenile assumptions of so many enthusiastic but undiscriminating enthusiasts who believe that a sports car must be hard work to master, to control, even merely to drive. According to popular assumption, a 'supercar' (whatever that may mean) ought to present even more difficulties. That is ridiculous: a supercar is not a supercar unless it is super in every respect. Simply to be faster or more accelerative or more stylish is not enough; it may be all of these things, but if it be a pain to park it, to negotiate a city in it, or to seek distant prospects in it, then the confounded thing is an infracar, not a supercar. If there be any such thing as a supercar at all, the NSX must be it, the one and only car to offer transcendent performance without demanding practical sacrifice. Can it make sense to buy a machine and then strive to do much of its work with your own muscle? Is there any good reason why only the young and strong and supple and perhaps athletically skilful should be able to realise the performance of which a supercar should be capable? A frail old lady, reliant only on experience and judgement, should be able to drive one just as well. In an age when brains, both real and electronic, have attained fingertip rule over as much power, as much precision, as much nicety of expression or forcefulness of impression as all man's rage and industry can muster, should it be hard to drive what purports to be the best of cars?

Setright, an Hassidic Jew who writes for quality British journals, almost thunders at times. You can imagine him writing 'We will fight them on the beaches' type speeches, can't you? Some may remember him testifying for Honda on TV commercials in the early 1990s. He had a beard like a burst mattress and was dressed entirely in black, and he boomed, 'In the year I began writing about cars Honda started making them.' The slogan was: 'Honda. The fear of Europe.'

He is absolutely right about the NSX. Certainly there are

probably other 3-litre V6 road cars that can attain 270 km/hr. There are other very worthy supercars. But I know of none that you climb into like your favourite old jersey and just potter about in if you want to. I know of none so welcoming, so easy to live with, so unfussy, yet when you are ready, so awesomely athletic and willing.

The late Ayrton Senna put it like this: 'Many other sports cars you can only drive a couple of days a week because they are too rough, heavy and noisy. The NSX is different.'

For this writer, no car has ever been so forgiving at speed. On the Motegi circuit in Japan I had this car up to speeds I can scarcely believe myself. I got to the point of leaving my braking later, getting closer to each corner before slowing. Eventually, and making sure there was no other car close to me as I did so, I tried the no-no of braking on the apex. The car performed a slight fishtail action, regained its composure and straightened up. This was forgiveness to a level I have never before known at speed. This was the legacy of a company that knows about balance as a motorcycle manufacturer would. That mid-mounted rear engine was right where it should be to prevent imbalance and pendulum forces. Shortly after that, something happened elsewhere on the circuit and the safety car came out and slowed us all down for a few laps. Suddenly, at these slower speeds, I could have been in a Honda Accord or Civic, so docile had the beautiful NSX become.

The NSX was launched on the world market in 1991. The fact that at one stage it reached over $200,000 in price meant that only a handful sold in New Zealand. A few have been imported second-hand. I suppose one day in the year 2010, I'll come across one for sale by the side of the road or in some grotty Park'n'Sell. And I will say to myself, 'How could you ever have fallen in love with something that looked like that?' The way one does with Triumph Stags. And the Honda NSX might well find voice and reply as I walk away, 'You're not so flash yourself these days.'

The Jaguar XK8 Coupe which was introduced in 1996 and commercially launched in 1997 was another leap forward for sports cars. Mind you, Jaguar owed us something. Do you remember what may have been the most classically beautiful sports car ever built, the Jaguar E Type? And do you remember the sinfully artless barge of a thing that Jaguar replaced it with? The XJS? Its designers should have been towed behind it for five kilometres.

Mind you, here we have a company that has had more owners than you could shake a dipstick at. They include the British Government, which in itself means one must have sympathy. Today, lucky for it, Jaguar is owned by Ford. This gives it access to development finance, R and D, and purchasing discounts from component suppliers on a scale Jaguar could never before dream of. In my view, this has saved the company. Under Ford stewardship Jaguar has not only survived, it has come up with a new family of cars that are world class in every respect. Ford has since bought Volvo. Its influence on the Swedish marque will be interesting to watch.

I remember times in the 1970s when I declined to take test Jaguars home, knowing they would drop oil in my driveway. Jaguars were the oil crisis. Quality control and reliability was questionable. The company was living on its name. The company's charming CEO of the late 1990s, Nick Scheele, freely admitted all that when I was chatting to him one night in Perth.

'We knew we had to completely rebuild the company, Peter. And we knew that we had one chance to get it right.'

They did.

The 4-litre XK8 family of sports cars and the current crop of Jaguar saloons are a credit to the new Jaguar company, and a pleasure for any driver to experience.

My first test drive of the XK8 was of several pre-launch models in the environs of Perth late in 1996. I was there with a small number of other motoring journalists. I was sitting at the wheel of one of the convoy of XK8s outside the front door of the hotel waiting for my co-driver, Neil Nelson of Palmerston North, to join me for the start of the event. He did not come. Everyone switched off their engines, and a search of the hotel was mounted. Sadly, Neil had died of a heart attack during the night.

We continued with the test drive programme because we knew that's what Neil would have wanted. We know, too, he would have agreed with us that it was a very competent car indeed.

When it comes to the Italian sports cars, I find I enjoy today's crop of Fiats and Alfas more than the big-name stables. The 1998 Fiat Turbo Coupe is gob-smackingly fast and gyroscopically stable. It is rare for me to pick up my cellphone and call a car company to congratulate them on their car from right there in the driver's seat. But I did just that with the 5-cylinder 2-litre Fiat Turbo Coupe in late 1998.

Quite separate from the Fiat's performance was the charming way the company had reintroduced retro features from the '50s. The fascia was of painted metal. When did you last see a slab of painted metal running across a car's fascia, adorned with chromium script announcing the name of Pininfarina, the car's stylists? The petrol filler cap was a large chromium affair, and the accelerator pedal had holes bored in it redolent of cruder vehicles of earlier days.

Like Jaguar, the Italians tested the world's patience in terms of quality control. Italian cars always had lashings of style and tons of go. But you could watch an Italian car rust before your very eyes in the '70s and early '80s. One group of American owners got so angry they took out a class suit. Assembly could be slapdash. And there were always strange warning lights coming on for no reason, and little bits of wiring hanging down or sticking out. You got the feeling that your car was made the day of the big football match and it had been hurried through so that everyone could go to the game.

But in the mid-1990s Fiat and Alfa Romeo (same company)

picked up their act. Like Jaguar they went from being sub-standard to well above acceptable standard. Proof was that in 1998 an Alfa Romeo saloon, the gorgeous 156, won the prestigious title of European Car of the Year, an accolade awarded by 56 senior motoring writers from throughout Europe.

What Did You Do Before You Had Central Locking, Uncle?

I always measured the quality and future prospects of early girl-friends by whether they were prepared to lean over and wipe the inside of the windscreen in front of me so that I could see out through the condensation. One in three or four would, without bidding, produce a delicate hankie or a sleeve and considerately wipe a hole through which I could see and navigate. Such a woman was highly likely to be asked out a second time.

By this time I had moved on from the Singer SM1500 to a badge-engineered Gazelle. My 1959 Singer Gazelle was a Hillman Minx with additional chromium trim on the outside and smarter looking seats plus woodgrain trim on the inside. The year I bought it was 1969. As with so many cars then, it had no heater. There was nothing to demist the front and rear screens. It travelled on narrow cross-ply tyres. Brakes and steering did not benefit from power assistance. And the floppy column change was, one again, like a withered arm.

In damp or cold conditions, we wiped and smeared to see out of the car.

Everyone kept an old tea towel or ruptured pair of jocks in the glovebox for the purpose. I kept a pair of panties in the glovebox, because this produced a reaction which said 'He's either a stud, or he's got style.' Neither was true. But I enjoyed the effect.

Windscreen washers were also something one had to fit. This would entail installing a plastic bottle under the bonnet, and running tubing from it to the jets and to a plunger button inside the car. You needed to plunge the plunger button 48 times before you saw the first few droplets of cleansing liquid dribble dejectedly out of the jets and down the bonnet. Getting up enough force to actually deliver the liquid onto the glass was a job for which you needed a wall-planner.

In the cars of the '50s, '60s and early '70s, we would apply our brakes judiciously in damp conditions. The skinny cross-plies offered a miserably small contact patch with the road. Some cars still had cable-operated brakes which could suddenly conjure up a vicious imbalance of braking effort due to a stretched cable, with the result that the car could skate in any direction.

We would fit all kinds of strange devices that relied on rubber suction cups or stick-on silver paper that we tapped into the electrical system and that were supposed to heat the window glass to prevent condensation. They had a limited effect and they were all made by someone called Smiths. Blacksmiths? Goldsmiths? Silversmiths? The label simply said Smiths. Very occasionally today, you may still see an old car on which the stick-on silver paper rear demister unit is hanging by a thread.

Every car had a pull-out choke for use when cold-starting. It provided a richer ratio of fuel to air to help fire the engine into life. You needed to learn precisely how much choke was required or risk flooding the carburettor with petrol and having to wait for it to evaporate in order to achieve a reasonable air/fuel ratio again. One woman I know admitted that she found the choke control very handy to hang her handbag on. I don't expect you to believe that for one second. But I happen to know it to be true. Her fuel consumption must have been phenomenal.

A car parked outside in very hot weather could suffer from something called vapour lock. Fuel sitting in a fuel line would turn to vapour in the ambient heat. This caused a bubble in the fuel line that stopped the fuel pump delivering a constant stream of liquid fuel to the carburettor and the car would not start. Nuisance though this was, it was useful as an excuse when you received a parking ticket. It was always vapour lock and 'thus I was unable to remove the car'.

When I look at today's cars I wonder how we managed back then. Rear screen demisters are embedded in the window glass. All cars have heaters which can be programmed to send warm air up the inside of the windscreen to clear it. A large proportion of cars have air conditioning, which means they have built-in dehumidifiers which keep glass clear of condensation. Head-lights are strong. Tyres are wide, fat and grippy. Most new cars have airbags. More expensive ones have airbags that come at you from every direction possible. (Hey, Peter, what's that rash you have on your face? Oh, I ran over the kerb at the supermarket and all the airbags went off in my Fiasco GLX. It's airbag rash.)

Today many cars have seatbelt pre-tensioners, devices that sense an impact and tauten the seatbelts before the body mass of the car's occupant reacts and thrusts forward. This prevents the injury that can occur when the body travels forward then is suddenly arrested.

ABS is fast becoming the norm. You can jam on the brakes and be reasonably sure that this will not turn the car into a sledge that will skid out of control.

The silicone chip is, as we all know, capable of carrying out functions hundreds of times per second, well beyond anything the human brain can perceive. In the case of ABS, the chip applies and releases the brakes many times each second. This stops the wheels completely locking up under panic braking. They go into braking mode, then back into turning mode, then back to braking mode. In the absence of lock-up, the driver can still steer the car, hopefully to a safe outcome. The beginnings of ABS are to be found in the aviation industry, where there was a need to stop airliners slewing off icy or wet runways when the brakes were applied after landing.

Added to ABS is traction control, which works in exactly the same way. A vehicle that is under power may lose traction in slippery conditions. The chip applies and releases power many times per second, thus stopping a wheel from slipping or skidding. More intelligent permutations of these systems have begun to appear, whereby power and braking effort can be controlled to correct any imbalance. If the car's sensors detect that one wheel is losing traction, braking can be applied to that wheel to prevent it spinning and worsening the situation. Applied to four-wheel-drive systems, this kind of intelligence allows either power or braking to be sent to any wheel that indicates it needs it, preventing potential loss of control.

In a vehicle fitted with all this, I no longer need to think. I can switch my brain power to the many problems and mysteries of the world we live in. Such as why the paper bags for the baguettes are always shorter than the baguette itself thus ensuring that by the time you get it home it is coated over one-third of its surface with bacteria. And why if the sign in the hotel says that check-out time is 10 a.m., absolutely everyone arrives at the cashier's desk at 10 a.m. And why the instant the airline makes the first boarding announcement, 96.2 per cent of passengers surge forward, pushing and shoving as they go.

If anyone asked me to name the five most significant inventions improving automotive safety and convenience in the last 30 years, my answer would be thus:

Vehicle air conditioning. The summers in New Zealand

and Australia are searingly hot and are becoming more so with global warming. Nothing makes a driver more aggressive than being hot. But air conditioning is not only about cooling. It is about almost instant clearance of condensation on window glass in winter or in humid conditions. Thus it is one of the best contributors to year-round safety there is. If it came to a choice between a/c and some smart stereo system, I would go for a/c any day.

I also believe that any employer who expects staff to drive fleet cars in Australia or New Zealand that are not air conditioned should expect a higher than normal accident rate and lower than normal performance from their employees. After all, air conditioning is standard in the rumpiest of used imports in New Zealand. In Australia, used imported vehicles are not a force to be reckoned with as the regulations there impose a huge duty on them. But some trade unions and workers' organisations have to a degree bargained with employers for vehicle air conditioning to be supplied as part of an industrial agreement.

Radial tyres. A change in the way tyre casings were woven, from a cross-ply pattern to a radial pattern, paved the way for wider and 'grippier' tyres, now universal across the industry. I 'lost' the Singer Gazelle one night on a fairly sharp bend on Shelly Beach Road which acts as an exit from Auckland's harbour bridge. Anne and I were concentrating on singing along with the song 'What's it all about, Alfie' on the scratchy car radio, which was a big-time song that year from some movie or other. As the Gazelle entered the right-hand bend in the rain, it simply let go at the back. We described a perfect 180-degree turn. The car was uncontrollable. Luckily there was no other traffic and we simply clipped a parked car.

This incident was a direct by-product of narrow cross-ply tyres trying to cope in a world that was getting faster. The Auckland City Council carved grooves in the road surface on that bend immediately afterwards. The reason? Apparently, what happened to us was almost a daily occurrence. The only factor that was not common to all the other incidents they had recorded on that bend was the song 'What's it all about, Alfie.'

I understood at the time that if the same song had been associated with the other mishaps on that bend, the Auckland City Council would have drafted and passed a bylaw rendering it illegal to listen to the song in a car within the boundaries of the city.

Central locking. Remember I am listing items of both safety and convenience here. This one is definitely a convenience item, and one that could all too easily be overlooked. Nothing was more a pain in the butt than having to lean all over the car, acquiring hernias and ruptures in the process, to lock each door separately. There you were, lying prostrate and looking most unappealing, as you reached to every corner of the compass to push down the locking buttons. There were things you would rather be doing, for sure.

The first time I saw central locking was on a Toyota Crown I was loaned in the very early 1970s. Like airbags, it took a very long time to become an industry norm. It is extraordinary how some inventions seem to constipate, and then get backed up some blind alley somewhere, to re-emerge twenty years later. Imagine life today without central locking. It has even been extended to the fuel filler flap and the boot or tail gate.

ABS. Anti-lock braking systems have saved, and will save, many lives. As the car comes more and more to be treated as just another home appliance, driving skills will diminish. Thus, technology must take over to protect the driver and his or her passengers. Anti-lock braking systems act to deter the car from entering an uncontrollable and potentially lethal skid.

Let me pass on a tip here that I gained from attending an Audi course in advanced driving. If in your ABS-equipped vehicle you need to make a panic stop, push that brake pedal right through the fire wall. Audi's research showed that many drivers thought that an initial jab on the brake pedal meant the

ABS took over, and pedal pressure could be released. Not so. In most ABS-equipped cars, you need to keep your foot to the floor for the ABS to continue to work. A few systems, such as Mercedes Benz's 'Brake Assist', will continue to help you even if you release pedal pressure. But how many of us drive very late model Benzes?

On the Audi programme, held at my own beloved Whenuapai airfield, I was asked to rush the car towards an obstacle, brake hard, and steer around it. I succeeded. But observing others carrying out the exercises, I quickly came to believe that to get the best out of ABS you have to hit it hard and stay on it until you are out of the Scheisen. Of course, hitting a brake pedal hard is anathema to many drivers. Why? Prior to ABS this is exactly what you did not do, unless you wanted to go into a lethal skid. In time, systems like Benz's 'Brake Assist' will become more common and no form of brain activity will be required. But for now, take care.

Power steering. This one is both a safety and a convenience item, and again, it could easily have been overlooked. I am well aware that the first power steering systems appeared in the US before or about the time I was born. But did they ever take a long time to get into cars being sold in Australia and New Zealand.

If you drove a medium- to heavyweight car you developed the arm muscles of a tugboat master — although even he got power steering on his vessel before you got it in your car. We wrestled and struggled with impossibly heavy steering mechanisms in Australasia, which contributed to stress and frustration. Both countries were a world away from the capitals of the car industry. Both countries tried to cobble together cars from parts sent from America or Britain, even Europe, although Holden and Ford in Australia came round to doing considerable work on producing an Australasian product.

But in both countries it seemed that cars were built-down to a price. No power steering. No air conditioning. In some cases, it was a matter of fitting your own after-market heater. It was as though acceptance of lower levels of equipment was part of being antipodean. After all, few of us had travelled and witnessed the high levels of equipment the Americans enjoyed in their cars.

We were still two nations at the end of the earth who were prepared to accept the idea that we were inferior and did not deserve extras in cars. And governments and car companies screwed us right royally. The lack of power steering in cars right up until the late 1980s is symbolic of this attitude.

In New Zealand, the arrival of imported second-hand cars brought Kiwis to the realisation that Mr and Mrs Hakamoto in Tokyo enjoyed power steering, power windows and air conditioning even in a humble 1-litre car. But Australia effectively blocked used imported cars by imposing a massive import duty on them, so Australians did not get to see the high levels of equipment that were fitted to some of these vehicles. It is not an issue now. Time has moved on. Customers are more demanding. Competition is keener. And all car manufacturers offer high levels of equipment.

It is true to say that there have been other inventions and innovations that have in their own small way contributed to better cars and better driving.

They are easily overlooked, I guess, except by motoring writers whose job is to observe and take stock. Because they have arrived quietly, because you cannot recall what preceded them, and because you may not have been born then anyway, some that I mention may surprise you.

The day/night rear vision mirror comes to mind. I first discovered it on an early 1970s Fiat. It was also on a Fiat (a gorgeous 125 Coupe) that I first discovered a five-speed manual gearbox. Now all manuals are five-speed, and on high-performance cars like top-end Alfas and BMWs you will find six-speed boxes. The ignition key system that is also a steering column lock was another great advance. It increased the degree of difficulty involved in stealing a car to the point where I gave up the occupation completely.

Versatile seat adjustment mechanisms, whether manual or electric, have also been helpful. I have the misfortune to be oddly shaped. This has not gone well in either the Piper Tomahawk or 3000 cars. Using the old Brass Monkey scale, I have five feet seven inches of head and torso, and one-and-a-half inches of leg. Anne is not all that ergonomically easy, either. She is five feet and two inches, although fairly evenly distributed between top and bottom. She will always haul a seat seriously forward. Should I go to get into a vehicle freshly vacated by Anne, I almost de-knacker myself as I tumble into it, so close to all the sharp bits has she left the seat adjustment.

Near the end of 1998, a friend of ours needed a new car. Her early 1980s Volvo was dying, in fact it was in rigor mortis. (Good Lord. The Bill Gates spellcheck just changed rigor mortis to Roger Morris. 'I am sorry. She had been dead for some days before being discovered. She was suffering from the effects of Roger Morris.') Anyway, replacement of Peggy's car was both urgent and my job. I sent her out in a number of good cars, all of which were given the thumbs-down. These were very good cars indeed. When I delved into the reasons, it turned out that none of them could provide a very short person with a comfortable driving position. Peggy never said as much. But what she did say got me asking questions of myself. I guess the degree in psychology must count for something. Having worked a few things out, I was quickly able to find her a car that would make her comfortable — a 1996 model Holden Vectra. It comes down to looking and listening. This is something every motor dealership salesperson should be trained in. Too many salespeople want to push their own agenda (sales target) onto the customer, regardless of the customer's needs.

One thing you do not see, but which is commonplace today, is the catalytic converter that reduces air pollution. Saab ran an experiment in London in which it measured the dirtiness of the air going in through the car's grille, and the gases coming out the exhaust pipe of the Saab. The company was able to demonstrate that what came out of the exhaust pipe was cleaner than what went into the car's air intake.

On the flipside of this coin, though, the car industry also has much to be modest about. In the rush to make the car safer and more user-friendly, there have been some appalling omissions.

One that concerns me is that despite the many innovations we have seen, on most cars one must still lean in over a dirty engine to check the oil and grub around on the ground to check tyre pressures. And the way car audio has developed is, to my mind, almost criminal. A good-sized knob and a row of chunky function buttons that one could operate by Braille have been replaced in many cars by an audio head that looks like a pin cushion. It is strewn with tiny buttons the size of tack heads, labelled in nine-point type that no-one can read in poor light. If you are moving from one car to the next as I do, you get to the point where you don't bother with audio. Every audio head is laid out differently. Just finding the power switch to turn the thing on requires a fairly dedicated search party. Switching from FM to tape to CD requires a doctorate. I prostrate myself at the shrine of Honda and Lexus and two or three others who have shunned this stupidity and provide simple audio heads with controls that are easy to see, read and feel. I well appreciate that today's car audio systems are very sophisticated and there is a need to include a lot of controls in a very small space. Well, if a few car makers can successfully insist that their audio suppliers keep it simple and therefore safer, why can't they all? In my view, the manufacturers of many of today's car audio systems are those who have contributed least to road safety.

The other major atrocity in the car industry, which I have already mentioned in earlier chapters, is the lack of standard positioning for major controls. If you rent a car or, as I do, find yourself driving several different cars every week, you can fumble from left to right, activating windscreen wipers when you want indicators and indicators when you want windscreen wipers. It should not be so.

In the late '80s and early '90s Honda came up with a fairly strange idea. You sat in an Accord or a Legend, and found in front of you a slot marked 'Coin'. My immediate reaction was 'Bloody hell'. You have just bought the thing, now you have to put money in to make it go. It turned out that Honda had incorporated a small cupboard in which those who had to drive on toll roads and toll bridges could store their coins. In Tauranga, New Zealand and Brisbane, Australia, toll bridges speed one to the airport for a very reasonable fee. In both places, they have a toll bridge that is so well designed and cuts off so many driving kilometres on the way to the airport that I am happy to pay the money.

The question, and it is a fair one, is how many times round are we being asked to pay? We finance the roading network from petrol and other taxes. Yet still we read of plans to turn roads and bridges into user-pays arrangements.

Years ago when the Auckland Harbour Bridge was a toll bridge the motorbike gangs used to make their opposition to the toll plain. The leather-gloved bikies used to plant a two-bob coin, then known as a florin, on the cylinder head of the bike before joining the bridge freeway. As you can imagine, it got fairly hot. A bit more than fairly hot. When they arrived at the toll gates they removed the coin with their leather-gloved hands and tossed it, incandescent, into the toll collector's bare-fleshed and ungloved hand. I am not suggesting I approve of this, but it does illustrate how passionate people can get about the user-pays mentality.

I was about to remark that in the '70s rubber cam belts used to snap. They still do, but not nearly as often. Your average used import Honda will throw a cam belt at about 80,000 km. The fact that on some used imports the odometer reads 39,000 km when this happens is another issue. But a belt failure at 80,000 km is, in my view, indicative of reasonable wear and tear.

Low-mileage belt failures were common in the late '60s and early '70s, especially on Fiats. Componentry in those days was not great. Neither was the path that a belt had to run. Serious and devoted women had to give up their hosiery in the cause. There was nothing like a length of rumpity old pantyhose for stretching over the fan pulley, and the water pump and generator pulleys of a snapped Standard Ten, although there was somewhat more erotic interest to be had in the days of separate stockings. ('I think the left one will get us home, Linda.') But pantyhose made a very good temporary fan belt, even though the car leapt two metres into the air every time the big knotty bit came round.

DETOUR

I guess if something like this is going to happen, it will happen at the Paris Motor Show.

It was the second of two press and trade days that preceded the public opening of the show. There I was, one of a large horde standing admiring the new Porsche Boxster which had just been unveiled, when I felt a hand on my buttock.

Here I am, 20,000 km of jetlag away from home, jammed in among this teeming horde, and someone has got their hand on my buttock. Not only that, the hand has begun to move in a circular, caressing action.

Now a lot of things go through a man's mind at a time like this. The feeling is akin to the one you get when you hear something strange and suspicious at 4 a.m. Don't try to tell me that you don't do what I do . . . which is to lie there in quiet, frozen fear for a minute while plucking up the courage to investigate. Well, this buttock-grabbing situation was the same. I looked resolutely ahead at some of the finest lines Porsche had ever built into a car. The hand continued its labour of love. I cast a furtive glance to my immediate right. I saw a portly photographer, with a bushy beard and breath that smelt like a camel driver's armpit, taking a light meter reading in preparation for a shot of the car. Both his hands were visibly employed. I could only assume that he was from Poland, where they have not caught up with automatic exposure cameras yet.

To my immediate left was one of the many immaculately turned out motor show hostesses, all mini-skirt and blazer, who had obviously left her post to come to the Porsche stand for the unveiling of the beautiful new Boxster. I could not see her hands. But then this was a fairly densely packed crowd.

I continued to fix my gaze on the Boxster, the car with which Porsche would try to capture buyers who did not have quite as much to spend as the traditional Porsche buyer of the past. Its aesthetic qualities were beginning to fade. That corrupt old hard disk that serves as my brain told me I really needed to know whose hand this was, thus to decide whether I should be enjoying myself or not. The time had come. There was only one way to bring this matter to a head. Tightly packed though the crowd was, I forced one arm behind me and grabbed the hand of the buttock burglar. Unfortunately, this action caused the Polish photographer to go sprawling, tripod, camera bag, spare films and all, just as he was about to take the award-winning cover shot for some magazine doubtless called something like *Polksi Karski*. Until that time, I had no idea that the phrase 'F-ing son of a bitch' was Polish.

The beautiful mini-skirted and blazered one jumped about ten feet into the air. When she landed again her face was the colour of a stoplight.

'Oh, Monsieur. Excusez-moi.' She looked at her now reddened hand.

Oh dear, it seems as though I was enjoying myself after all.

I was able to communicate to her that my having learned French to sixth form level, and a long time ago at that, probably did not equip me for the ensuing conversation.

'Oh Monsieur. Je suis soh sorreee. My fiancé was standing ere weeth me looking at theese car. I did not realise that I 'ad lost eem.'

She then slipped away hurriedly into the throng in search of her boyfriend, who was clearly not the photographer, who had decided that a lying-on-his-belly shot was quite an arty idea after all.

Of Avoiding Gas Stations and Sports Cars

I loathe and detest having to stop at a gas station. I have done so all my life. I will run with the red fuel warning light on for days. This is a stupid practice. I may run out of fuel one day in an awkward place, and become a danger to traffic.

The inane questions that one gets asked do not help my mood. 'Can I check your oil and water, sir?' I say that they are fine thanks. What I really want to say is, 'How can you possibly check the sump oil level in an engine that has just been turning at 3000 rpm for the last three and a half hours? Do you suppose that the oil detaches itself from 25 engine components scattered all over the engine block and the timing gear, and lands back in the sump in one great plop in a frigging nanosecond? Don't you know that the only accurate way to check the oil level in an engine is to do so when the engine is cold?'

But I do not confront the gas jockeys with my indignation because they are, after all, just hard-working kids, and most of them are on about 15 cents an hour, with employers who resent them even going to the loo. A friend at an oil company tried to tell me that some very high-quality engine oils do drain back into the sump instantly. Pull the other one, Murray.

Then there is the fact that gas stations have turned into supermarkets. Now, I don't mind that fact in itself. It is very convenient to be able to buy all sorts of necessities at all sorts of hours at almost any gas station. The problem is that, unlike supermarkets, many gas stations have only one checkout, two if you are very lucky. So here you are, waiting to pay for your 50 bucks worth of gas, eighteenth in a line of people buying eggs, pies, tampons, disposable nappies, girlie magazines, boylie magazines, flowers, firewood, and rotisseried chickens. And don't even think of asking for a long-reach NK8-model spark plug or a teflon distributor cap.

And of course anyone of the female persuasion will wait until she gets to the very front of the queue and has had all her items added up by the cashier, before she will even think of opening her purse and beginning the long search for some cash or her plastic card.

Speaking of plastic cards, in 1998 Anne and I toured Tasmania in a supercharged Holden Commodore. Not one gas station we called at offered EFTPOS. And not one offered barcode scanning of our non-petrol purchases. In fact, in one little gas station on the outskirts of Hobart, the attendant actually took a pencil from behind his ear, licked the graphite end of it, wrote down the price of each item on the top bag of a pile of paper bags on the counter, and added them up manually.

At least I avoided having to tap my numbers into a keypad. Can you imagine the germs and bugs that must build up and be exchanged on those things? They are used by people with poor habits after visiting the toilet, patting the dribbling dog or changing the baby, to mention but a few hygiene evils. And what do we do? Use the keypad straight after them then immediately eat the sandwich we have just bought.

I have heard all the jokes that Australian mainlanders tell about Tasmanians. But there was a charm about this rather retro atmosphere that was almost engaging. There was a calmness about it that spoke of days when people had more time and less stress. I decided that far from being backward, Tasmanians may well know something about quality of life that other Australasians have forgotten.

The Tasmanians do not skimp on road building. Given its mountainous nature, Tasmania has some of the finest roads I have driven on anywhere in the southern hemisphere.

But back to my abhorrence of service stations. The problem of queues at service station counters became the subject of concern for at least one owner of a chain of New Zealand stations. They decided to install swipe-card mechanisms on their pumps, enabling customers who had only pulled in for fuel to pay by EFTPOS without needing to enter the building. Apparently the company later decided to limit the numbers of swipe-card pumps. The reason? They discovered that their sales of shop items had fallen considerably. People were not going into the building and were not being seduced by the confectionery, meat pies and magazines therein.

Citroën New Zealand's Bill Ritchie and I once decided to play a little trick on the staff of a large Auckland gas station. Bill and I knew that a Citroën BX, like other Citroëns that employed the company's gas-oil suspension system, was able to be driven on three wheels. This ability was the product of a combination of the fine balance inherent in the car, and the way the gas-oil suspension system would pump compensatory pressure around the car's extensive network of plumbing and gas spheres to keep it level.

Unnoticed by anyone, we removed the left rear wheel, the one nearest the fuel filler, in the service station's rear yard — we did this because we did not want to attract any problems with the law by driving the car on three wheels on the public road. We arrived at the pumps, where Bill wound down the driver's window and asked the young attendant to fill the tank. Round the back of the car the obliging boy went. Predictably, he was soon back at the driver's window, incredulous.

'Did you know your left rear wheel is missing?'

We admonished him for being silly and holding us up. How could a back wheel possibly be missing — we had just driven in here, had we not? How can you possibly drive a car on three wheels? The boy entreated us to get out and see for ourselves. We admonished him again, putting on an act of becoming mildly impatient. The boy continued to try to get us to look for ourselves. We told him that he was obviously suffering from delusions and that we had no more time to waste. We restarted the car and drove off . . . on three wheels . . . leaving the poor lad agape. No doubt he decided to swear off the Crunchie bars after that. We then quietly returned to the rear of the station and put the car back on all fours.

I know not whether it is a measure of my age, my gender, my strong sense of independence, my hatred of any kind of class or caste system, or some combination of these, but I cannot sit in a car while someone pumps the gas, then just hand over the correct money to the attendant and drive off. I concede that to do this is a very good way of avoiding all those queues, because you use the attendant to do the paying. But I like to pump my own gas. A recent survey by an oil company in New Zealand suggests that I am not alone. As many as one customer in three shares my preference.

I must say that in surveying the New Zealand urban scene, I note a pandemic of service stations. One stretch of major Auckland highway has six in less than two kilometres. It costs between $2.5 million and $5 million to establish an urban service station, from buying the bare land to selling the first pie or petrol. It is a little less in Australia, where the dollar is at a different level and real estate is often cheaper than in New Zealand. But one wonders how all these stations are going to remain profitable, particularly with the downward pressure on petrol prices. In my view, the service aspect will be the first to go from service stations. They may become totally self-service oriented, which suits me because I am well-practised at it. Or they may end up with one lane of pumps which has an attendant, but where the prices are higher than in the lanes where you serve yourself.

Not all oil companies have distinguished themselves in terms of environmental values when they have established these monoliths of plastic, neon and glaring colours. Many of them are a complete blot on the landscape. But I guess oil companies and environmental values are two things that are anathema to each other anyway.

As I drive through life, I am also reminded that gas stations are environmental deities compared to real estate companies. The real estate industry in New Zealand, and to a lesser extent in Australia, is guilty of the worst form of environmental atrocity in the way it peppers the landscape with the gaudiest signs imaginable. Not just one dazzling sign for each property for sale, but twenty. And not just on the property itself, but outside on the publicly owned grass verge. And not just outside on the publicly owned grass verge, but for several kilometres down the road, lest you should be unable to find the place. And not just delicate little signs. Huge psychedelic billboards that blot out the sun, blot out the senses.

New Zealanders are very ready to believe that we enjoy the world's best environment. This was correct when it was first planted into our heads decades ago by visiting overseas tourists. (Your country is so green and clean, the tourists all used to say.) Not any more. We have allowed the real estate industry to ruin it.

On Sundays, they emerge from all over and put extra signs and flags up everywhere, for Sunday is 'open home' day.

In fact, anyone who wishes puts up one or more of these huge, gaudy signs at the roadside to peddle their particular wares. And if we were such experts at preserving the environment, would we not remove the emergency vehicle sirens that disrupt the environment of our major cities every few minutes? Is it necessary for an emergency vehicle going from one part of a suburb to another to be heard in the seven surrounding suburbs? The only people who really need to hear a vehicle siren are the drivers of the vehicles immediately ahead of it — although some would argue that the shrill siren offers the victim some comfort, because he or she knows that someone is on the way.

If we were the environmental doyens of this planet that we think we are, would we allow people to have remote locking devices that crow and chirp like a cockerel when the key-tag remote lock button is pressed, disturbing or waking an entire suburb, just so that some desperately protective owner of a very ordinary car, or some overprotective courier driver, can be quadruply reassured that the vehicle is locked? Two or three flashes of the indicator lights will do the same job. That's the way the cars with factory-fitted security do it, such as BMW. And that is the way countries that really know about caring for the environment do it.

While we're on the subject of my preferences and prejudices, you may also be surprised to learn that soft-top sports cars aren't my favourite way to travel. Well, most of them, anyway. I have left this admission until late in the book out of concern that you may think I cannot be any kind of motoring journalist at all, given this particular affliction. The statement 'I hate sports cars' is not a categorical one. There needs to be some explanation, some definition, and I will attempt to provide these things.

We are all affected by associations, definitions and meanings that were significant in our developmental years. Therefore they have stayed with us. At that time in my life, a sports car was a wire-wheeled canvas-topped MG. Or it was a Morgan or an Austin Healey and others of that ilk.

I could not believe how crude, harsh and noisy these things were. I could not believe how difficult they were to get into, and how uncomfortable they were once you had achieved the task of getting into them.

In addition, they were never completely rainproof. There was always that little drip-drip-drip of cold water on that fleshy bit where the trouser cuff rides up from the top of the sock on your accelerator ankle. Drip-drip-drip. It's almost torture.

In Auckland's Karangahape Road one day in the 1970s, I sat at a red traffic light alongside a suitably scarfed and capped couple in a beautifully turned out Morgan Plus Four. As they waited for the lights to turn, they sat behind a cattle truck. What it was doing in the middle of the city I do not know. But it was fully laden with beasts. A bovine with an urge backed up to the tail gate of the truck and let forth a stream of green excrement not too different in shade from the British racing green of the Morgan. The stream of excrement cascaded right into the cockpit of the car. I would wager that the Morgan driver probably did not get the girl. And all my prejudices against so-called sports cars were not only confirmed, they were celebrated in liquid greenness.

I hate seeing animals squeezed into trucks like that. It seemed fitting that one had got its own back on someone. But I also recognise that the processing of these beasts is necessary to our economy. And I enjoy an occasional steak like so many other people.

I have been lucky. Except as a volunteer fireman, when we had to deal with nasty accidents involving death and disfigurement, I have not had to do a great deal of what might be termed 'dirty work'. Friends at university kept themselves financial by killing and cutting up cows, sheep and pigs at abattoirs. I can and have killed animals, mostly for humane reasons. But it would take me a while to become indifferent about it as must the abattoir worker, the culler or the hunter.

I have always fancied myself as a member of the military because I am from an air force family. Both my father and mother were enlisted, and I am the product of an air force affair.

I am now past the age where I would be asked to fly for my country. But I am pleased that we aviators have never had to look our prey squarely in the eyes. Today, I guess no warrior has to do that.

Anyway, you have lured me down a side road once again. I wish you would stop doing that. We were talking about sports cars.

My mother's maiden name is Kimber and she comes from a branch of the Kimber family of Oxford, England, who founded MG. My grandfather and several other relatives were employees of Morris Motors in Oxford, which acquired MG — MG stood for Morris Garages. This was a small enterprise that sold and serviced Morris cars, but it also developed its own line of sports cars using Morris components. My not being an aficionado of sports cars would probably be akin to treason were I to utter it in a pub in Cowley.

I think part of the problem was that I could never see where the sport came in. These cars, with their low centre of gravity and lightness of weight, were fine performers if you enjoyed track racing or hill climbs. But out on the roads, this way of travelling seemed onerous to me. Every truck that goes past deafens you. If the sun is out you get burnt so you have to put up the hood anyway; if it rains you get wet, so again you have to put up the hood, all of which seems to defeat the purpose somehow. When you park it somewhere you have to put up the hood for security.

And I feel compelled to say that the whole concept of enjoying 'sport' on today's public roads is a myth. The fastest you can legally travel on a public road in New Zealand is 100 km/hr. In Australia there are a few stretches where 110 is allowed. And these are generally straight stretches, of course. (Only in the Northern Territory can you really boot it. There are sections of road there with no speed limit.)

I know there are those who would argue that these limits are too low. But the legislators must take into account the abilities of those less skilled at driving than you or I, and the quality of the roads themselves. They must also look at the average speed that most people are comfortable driving at, and make sure the legal limit is not too far above that. To set the legal limit too far above the comfort zone is accident promoting in itself, for it causes situations where a few vehicles want to go much faster than the rest, and their drivers become frustrated trying to get through the traffic and begin to take risks.

It is my belief that the terms sports car, sporting handling, and sporting spirit are today owned by the advertising copy-writers. I do not believe these terms any longer have true meaning when applied to cars sold for use on the public road.

Is, for instance, a new BMW Three Series sedan adorned with sporty enhancements from the House of Schnitzer, or a Saab 9-3 coupe, any less of a sports car than a Mazda MX5 or an MGF? Is Jaguar's beautiful XK8 any more or less of a sports car than an Audi S8 sedan? Were this an interactive medium, I would be perfectly happy to listen to your thoughts on this. But this is old-fashioned, one-way, steam print. And no correspond-ence will be entered into. Which makes me feel wonderfully powerful, I might say.

How should we define a sports car today? I have driven many a saloon in the last few years that is the equal of a traditional sports car. The Alfa Romeo 156 easily fell into that category. Subaru's stunning WRX came very close, as did Ford's Escort Cosworth.

What I am suggesting is that the handling and performance that is built into today's cars creates saloons that suffer few penalties against sports cars, the principal of these being extra weight and higher centre of gravity. But at the same time, you can get a family into the saloons, and more than just a briefcase into the boot.

Another question I would like to set you thinking about is this: is a Toyota Celica GT4 hard-top any less of a sports car than an MGF or Mazda MX5? The Mazda and the MGF are principally open cars with folding canvas roofs, with clip-on hard-tops for those that require them. The Celica is a hard-top or coupe. I know which one I would rather campaign in when it comes to a spirited drive through the mountains on twisty, narrow roads. It would be the GT4 Celica complete with the tautness of body that a proper integral roof provides, and the added surety of foot that four wheel drive affords.

A car without a fixed roof is an interesting piece of physics. It is like a building that has four walls, but no roof to hold it taut. The roof of a car acts as a very important piece of bracing. With no roof, things start to shake. A vibration is set up throughout the car. You can't see anything in the rear view mirror because it is shuddering. So is the windscreen.

The car adopts a kind of mobile Parkinson's disease, reminiscent of those machines at Mitre 10 that shake up the tinting material in your four-litre can of paint. In the automotive industry, this phenomenon is known as scuttle shake. Every sports car and every convertible suffers from it to some extent, ranging in degree from very bad to reasonably under control. You can tell the owners of one that has very bad scuttle shake. They are the ones that get to the afternoon tea stop and can't drink their coffee because their hands are in such a tremor that the contents of the cup are launched in every direction.

Lengthy drives in a generation of convertibles and sports cars in late 1998 proved that scuttle shake is increasingly being brought under control. A Saab 9-3 Convertible, a Porsche Boxster, and a Jaguar XKR all demonstrated major advances in the reduction of scuttle shake.

Funny thing, but cars like the enormously successful Mazda MX5 sports car always look better to me when they are being driven by women. As a man, I have never felt comfortable about being seen in one. I cannot deny, however, that Mazda were very canny indeed in their decision in the late 1980s to produce this car. Whether I like two-seater soft-top sports cars or not, there are many who do. Mazda saw that the MG Midget and MGB had

gone. Austin Healey had gone. Two of the most popular suppliers of affordable two-seaters were no longer offering new cars.
Mazda jumped right in with a brilliantly designed, well-styled
car to fill the hole. What's more, it had a decent heater. And if
you really wanted it, you could have air conditioning to control
the climate when you had the roof up. It took the new owners
of the MG marque, Rover, six years to catch up. Rover, too, could
see a place in the market for a new two-seater sports car. Mazda
had leapt in and had reaped well-deserved sales rewards, but
Rover has the rights to the magical MG name. Rover launched
the MGF in the mid-1990s. With the engine mounted amid-
ships, the MGF possessed the classic sports car formula. The
closer to the central axis that you can concentrate weight, the
less pendulum effect that weight will have. It is like tying a stone
not to the end of a piece of string, as in a front- or rear-engined
car, but to the middle of the string. The MGF was and is a
brilliant car. But Mazda, with its front-engined MX5, offers a
prettier, more classic looking and better-built car. Mazda won
that round.

And yes, I have enjoyed driving Boxsters, MX5s, BMW, Saab
and even Benz pram tops. Of course I have. Anyone would whose
nerve endings still come to the surface. But they have been like
other people's kids. I look forward to giving them back.

Speaking of sports cars and convertibles, Anne and I were
assaying a BMW Three Series Convertible for a week when on a
sunny Saturday afternoon we fetched up in Warkworth, a small
and charming town about 50 minutes north of Auckland.

For us Warkworth has always been a real town. It is not one
of those towns with a mirror on a pole at each end to make it
look twice as big. It is not a whistle-stop town that people
charge right through without even noticing that it has a 'Do-It-
Yourself Massage Parlour'. Warkworth has natural substance of
its own, because for many years it has been just off the main
highway.

Towns that are just off the main highway are always much

more interesting than those through which the road passes. We found the same in Tasmania and in England, and I suspect it is the same everywhere. Towns just off the main highway can develop without deafening noise; their residents can cross the road in reasonable safety; and those motorists who do visit have made a conscious decision to visit the town and are therefore of higher quality than your zap-through 'let's-stop-for-a-milk-shake-and-go-deaf-while-we-drink-it' ordinaries.

So, we fetched up in just such a town, Warkworth. We had been driving in wind-in-the-hair mode and desperately needed to wet our whistles. The only parking space that seemed to be available was right in view of a revelling mob on the first floor balcony of a pub. I pressed the button that would raise the canvas roof. With balletic function and much whizzing of little hidden motors, the roof emerged from its concealed box just ahead of the boot. It whizzed and curtsied and pirouetted through the first half of the choreography. It pointed skywards, then forwards. It retracted a bit, and then moved forward. Then, it pointed skywards again. Then, it stuck solid. It froze in time and space, pointing skywards like a rocket launcher, refusing to go backwards or forwards.

Of course the revellers on the first floor balcony had been observing all this. It was entertainment they could not get if they paid for it. A couple of yuppies in a convertible BMW from the big smoke with their wanky flop-top, and the thing had seized.

They booed. They cheered. They threw half-eaten squid rings down at us.

They were having the time of their lives. And we were not.

At no time did I more sorely miss a proper car with a proper roof.

DETOUR

I met up with another of my old motoring writer mates, Seymour Titt Junior, when I was in California the other day for the world media launch of the Volvo C5 Coupe. Which, I might add, is a gorgeous vehicle, powered by one of the nicest 4-cylinder turbo engines in the world. Seymour would be 75 in the shade now. The nuggetty old motor-noter with a lunarscape of a visage and a bright red pincushion of a nose had lost none of his gnarly worldliness. He took one look at the Volvo and bulletined loudly, 'Friggin' Swedes are as silly as turnips. Spend so much time shaggin' and doin' weird things with birch branches and steam that they clear forget how to do their sums, man. This here engine is short by at least one cylinder, man.'

But he decided he would take it for a test run anyway, since he had come all the way from Falling Reputation, Idaho, for the event.

Seymour was, as always, worried that he'd get hungry on the drive route. He wrapped several potatoes in garlic-buttered tin-foil. He jammed the little silver parcels among the exhaust manifold plumbing of the engine, and proceeded to drive the entire test route in the mountains behind Santa Barbara at 5800 rpm in second gear. He stopped only when the aroma of roast spud became too much to resist. Whereupon he lifted the bonnet, and removed the repast, potato by potato, on the end of a knitting needle. He then proceeded to have a right royal roadside feed.

Surely It's What's Under the Bonnet that Counts

The above statement has much going for it. But it is not a complete truism.

I have known many cars, admittedly cars of the '50s, '60s and '70s, that had magnificently athletic engines, but which were woefully lacking in terms of brakes, suspension and handling.

In their day, they were known as the Muscle Cars. They had V8 engines. But they also had steering that was arranged on the old maritime system where you had to ring down your command to below decks and await a response.

They had brakes that felt like those little rubber blocks that rubbed against the wheel rim of your bike, and were about as effective. They had handling that said 'aim this car because there ain't no way you're gonna steer it'.

And all of us who were car nuts in that era know precisely which cars these were. And in which countries they were made, or rather quarried.

No manufacturer gets away with that now.

But under the bonnet, there has been one theme that has survived and endured. It has been a survivor that has fought off many predators. I speak, of course, of the V8 engine. My best efforts at research suggest that Ford was the first to introduce this format to the mass market. This is not to say that the Ford engine was the first ever V8. That argument is one which a sensible person stays clear of, and which matters little anyway. My vote goes with the people who make, market and successfully sell a product, rather than those who invent it. You should see the number of things that I have invented, including a rotisserie-format dog-washing machine. But no-one will take it to the market.

Where were we? Oh, yes. The year was 1932. The engine was a 3.6-litre 70 brake horsepower unit. And for many Americans, it was the first time they had seen, experienced or driven a V8 engine. Effectively, this was two four-cylinder engines tipped on an angle that roughly resembled a V shape, and which supplied energy to a single crankshaft in the bottom of the engine. Why was such a format devised? Because a straight-eight engine meant a row of cylinders that occupied enormous length. Manufacturers had offered straight eights, even straight twelves. But the realisation had dawned that these formats meant cars had to be the length of canal barges. This was not good for handling. And it meant that the bodies were so large they were stupendously expensive to make.

In an indulgent and invincible America, recovering from a stock market crash and wishing to look more frugal without actually being so, the V8 engine that afforded huge power but needed a much shorter bonnet was de rigueur.

Any eight-cylinder engine is challenged in times of fuel shortages. World War II was such a time, although the engine had military applications to which fuel rationing did not apply. Military vehicles of American persuasion went right on using the lusty V8.

125

But came the first oil shock of circa 1974, and the world pretended that large engines and large cars had leprosy. But every car enthusiast had a V8 in the barn or garage just waiting for the day of liberation. And it came.

I would not class myself as a V8 fan. But what I see and must help celebrate is this. Here is a very special engine format that has survived for something approaching 70 years. Yes, so have several other engine formats, but none so indulgent, so incredibly macho, so completely ignorant of today's priorities in terms of the preservation of fossil fuels, as the V8.

And do you know, there is no sound so pheremonal, so completely and absolutely engaging, as that of a V8 engine on song. There is something about eight cylinders arranged in a V. You do not get the same experience from four, six, or twelve cylinders laid out in V format. Eight is the magic number. There is a mathematical harmonic that in my view could form the subject for a doctorate for some bored academic. He or she could perhaps explain — using taxpayers' funds and maybe some financial support from Holden or Ford — what it is about the sound of a V8 engine that so engages the senses.

These engines are still with us after all this time. And agree with me or not, but they have a wonderful way of laughing, cackling, almost mocking. It is that roughish note that they exude, that clatters and chatters as it works. It laughs and giggles and gossips at the same time as it delivers extraordinary power.

Listen to a jetboat roaring up a river valley. What do you hear? Echoing off the walls of the canyon, you hear the percussive rasp, the chatter-chatter, of a V8 engine.

Although I am not by choice a V8 driver, something about that sound engages with the hormones and sets them into some kind of begging mode.

All this noise in the river valleys and canyons may not be a good thing to impose on the environment, I admit. But the power of that engine has helped many a Kiwi and similarly many a tourist to appreciate our dramatic rivers. And let's give a little pat on the back while we are at it. The jetboat propulsion system which is now used all over the world was arguably invented by a Kiwi, C.W.F. (Bill) Hamilton. His preferred engine? A V8.

In very recent times, Anne and I discovered that the V8 engine was alive and well in speedboat racing. One recent Easter we booked a cabin at the Green and Blue Lakes, near Rotorua. We got to the lakes to find that seemingly miles of lakefront road had been cordoned off with that tape the military police use to make them feel part of the real world. (OK, Corporal. We are placing 24-hour surveillance on Private Smith. We are fairly sure he is the one that's nicking the instant coffee.) Our lakeside camping ground was walled off by dirty brown scrim-type material that cut off our view of the lake, and the view of many others on the lake edge too. We had gone there to spend a quiet Easter. The campsite people had taken our deposit without telling us that a bunch of petrol heads would wall-off our view of the lake with scrim, and then spend hours and hours racing about in overpowered boats. The scrim was to stop those who had not paid from seeing the event.

These boat people proceeded to ruin what was to have been an intimate weekend, with a view of 40 acres of sacking between us and the lake, and incredible roaring sounds that seemed to go on all weekend.

My point, though, is that many of the engines in the boats were definitely V8s. I could tell by the sound. There is nothing like it, nothing so loin-stirring. Nothing lasers a beam to a man's visceral being like the throb, the rasp, the cackle of a V8.

V8s, after all these years, are still engaging. They have always fought for survival. Wars, oil crises . . . and now we witness the politically correct move towards electric cars, and hybrid petrol/electric cars. Still and all, a few car companies continue to offer the V8.

For how long is anyone's guess. The V8 was always a product of the indulgence of Americans. In the last two or three years the top-selling cars in the US have been V6s, some of them Japanese V6s. Cars like the Honda Accord, Toyota Camry and Ford Taurus have begun to conquer America. Enjoy the V8 while you still can. It is living on borrowed time.

Quite a different story surrounds the fortunes of the diesel engine. Not much more than a decade ago, most Australians and New Zealanders regarded diesel engines as noisy, smelly things that belonged in trucks and tractors. Despite the fact that in Europe and in the North American continent diesel-powered cars have enjoyed considerable patronage since the late 1960s or early 1970s, no self-respecting Aussie or Kiwi was prepared to give one garage-room. We were too fond of spirited acceleration, high speed and smooth running. In the northern hemisphere, buyers were prepared to trade those virtues against the fact that diesel cars were very good cold-weather cars. Having no carburettors or spark plugs, they were less prone to the vagaries of climatic extremes than petrol engines were. The Volkswagen Rabbit diesel was an extraordinarily popular car in Canada and North America for this and other reasons.

Tests of gas turbine engines in cars conducted by both British and US concerns did not result in anything mass market-able. Rover and Chrysler did good work. But it was the kind of work that said No rather than Yes.

A gas turbine engine is what, in aviation terms, we loosely know as a jet prop or turbo prop engine. It powers all manner of passenger airliners, as well as military heavyweights such as Hercules and Orions. The engine works in the following way. First it takes in air and compresses it, then the air is heated by the combustion of fuel, which causes it to rapidly expand and try to force its way out of the combustion chamber. In doing this, the air pushes on the blades of the turbine. The turbine spins and turns a shaft which, in the case of an aeroplane engine, drives a propeller, and in the case of a car, the wheels. Because the energy it produces is already in rotary form, this type of engine is very powerful, and its performance is silky smooth. In an ordinary reciprocating engine, the piston climbs up the cylinder, stops, and then reverses its direction as it is forced back down the cylinder again. This push/pull up/down action has to be converted, via connecting rods and a crankshaft, into the rotary movement needed to drive the wheels.

Modern cars are far smoother running than those of decades ago. This is due to better flywheel and crankshaft design, the use of counterweights, and all sorts of other trickery which takes the lumps and bumps out of engine action. But the reciprocating internal combustion engine will never achieve the gossamer smoothness of the turbine. Chrysler and Rover both noticed these advantages.

The first car to be equipped with a gas turbine engine was a Plymouth Belvedere, in 1954. It produced a creditable 100 horsepower but its fuel economy was considered poor. Chrysler Corporation, of which Plymouth was part, produced a second engine in 1959. It was double the horsepower of the first. After some experimentation, Chrysler decided to build 50 turbine-powered cars and give them to the American public to test drive. There was a huge clamour of volunteers — 30,000 in all. The idea was each driver would use the car for a few months, make a full report on it, and pass it on to someone else. By 1966, just over 200 people had driven the Chrysler Turbine Fleet. But many were unhappy with its fuel consumption and the lag time between idle and full power. Meanwhile, on the other side of the Atlantic, Rover had come to much the same conclusion. All eyes were now on the emergence of another type of rotary engine, the Wankel, which had a large revolving solid rotor and produced phenomenal power with none of the lag of the turbine, even though it was a little greedy on fuel. Mazda had acquired rights to further develop and build this car, and it was enormously successful for a number of years, until sales were affected by the oil shocks of the 1970s.

Meanwhile, no-one was more surprised than the Kiwi or Aussie tourist of the 1970s and 1980s when they fetched up in

Singapore and found that the entire public transport system was a huge fleet of taxis, all of which were diesel powered and many of which were carrying the three-pointed star of Stuttgart. Yes, diesel-engined cars were being manufactured by the world's most prestigious car makers. But there was no way an Aussie or a Kiwi was prepared to accept that something that powered a tractor or a fishing boat could properly and decently propel a car.

In 1992, Citroën importer Mike Apthorp decided to take a punt in the New Zealand market. Although Mercedes Benz and a couple of others had imported a few diesels for diesel nutters, the Citroën importer decided to go for broke on it. Peugeot/ Citroën (a marriage that I wish had never happened because it has deprived Citroën of its individuality) made one of the best diesel engines in the world, which powered the BX range of Citroën cars. Mr Apthorp knew it was a stunning package. He knew that the cheapness of the fuel would appeal to Citroën owners, given that they tended at the time to be muesli-munching, kaftan- and sandal-wearing tree-huggers.

I drove a 1.9-litre BX diesel from Auckland to Wellington; it was something over 700 km. Ignoring for the moment the quite low road-user tax paid at that time by the operators of diesel vehicles in New Zealand, it cost me just over $17 at the pump to make that journey, and to make it in a very spacious and comfortable car.

Citroën diesels took off in the marketplace. A year later, a dozen makers were offering diesel alternatives in the antipodean marketplace. Today, it is a matter of who doesn't offer a diesel rather than who does.

In my view, the biggest advance in making the diesel engine acceptable is the marriage of diesel and turbocharging. Turbo diesels now perform as athletically as some petrol engines. Manufacturers have also learned how to silence them.

The four-wheel-drive pandemic has also improved the fortunes of the diesel engine. Few of the image-seekers and pretenders who have bought these vehicles could afford the petrol bills that go with hauling around the kind of wasteful tonnage they are now responsible for. The availability of a diesel engine helps keep it affordable.

It does not seem all that long ago that the diesel pump was round the back of the gas station. You had to paddle about in this large, black pool of gungy crude, fighting off Kenworths and Macks; your hand smelled of diesel all day, so sticky and icky was the pump handle. Which meant your sandwiches came to smell of diesel. You soon learned that the odour that transferred onto you from the pump handle did nothing for women. They preferred a fragrant something from Pierre Cardin, or in my language, Mr Peter Cardigan.

The engine of the future looks like being a combination of internal combustion and battery-electric. Let us all enjoy ourselves before such an aberration becomes boringly compulsory.

Over the decades, I have had all kinds of engine inventors approach me for publicity, most of them pushing some kind of variation on the rotary theme. The Australian Sarich engine has seemingly been in danger of being fitted to a mass production line of vehicles for decades. But no-one has taken the risk on any meaningful scale.

As for the four-wheel-drive Outback, I think I can explain. For years, we antipodeans have been denied big vehicles at affordable prices. Competition in Australia, and a deregulated market in New Zealand, means that vehicles that may have cost a person three times their annual income five or ten years ago now cost maybe one year's income. My good mate, the Kiwi Male, has plunged deeply into the macho vehicle thing. He wants one that is huge and commanding.

Talking of macho, remember the days when we used to do our own oil changes? I was reminded of this the other day as I watched a young woman pouring four litres of oil into her EB2 Honda Civic. I have seen her quite often in the basement carpark of the building in which I work. I guess pouring in four litres is one way of doing an oil change. At one stage, I used to do mine in a deep stormwater ditch outside my house. It was possible to drive the vehicle over the ditch so that the right-hand wheels were parallel with one side of the excavation, and the left-hand wheels were parallel with the other. This allowed me to lie in the ditch on my back and have plenty of room to undo the sump nut and manoeuvre a container under the engine to catch the exiting oil. In the winter, I had to put on a wetsuit. One day, while lying on my back in the wetsuit in 25 centimetres of water, I heard sirens approaching. First one, then a second. They did not go past. Next thing three faces in peaked caps peered under the car. This happened at the very nanosecond that I was releasing the sump nut. I became distracted and the sump dropped its entire contents on my head. 'Hallo,' hailed one of the hats. 'You're OK, then.'

'Except for four litres of oil on my head, I guess I'm OK.'

Said the hat, 'If you don't mind our asking, what are you doing lying in a stream under this vehicle in a wetsuit? Are you having a bath? Do you have a rubber fetish? Is there a full moon tonight? Are you saving the whales?'

'I'm changing the oil.'

Said the hat, 'I see. It's just that we had a call from a passing truck driver to say that he thought there had been an accident. It's the legs sticking out from underneath the vehicle, you see.'

At this I sat bolt upright, in the process whacking my head on the sump guard. Hard. Just then a disturbed eel slid over my nether regions. I've not changed my own oil since.

And the legacy of the head injury is still with me. Occasionally I have visions that the AA has become a travel agent and a purveyor of mail-order alarm clocks and suitcases that attract Fly Buys points. If you hit your head as hard as I did, such delusions are understandable.

DETOUR

This court is now in session. The first case is the people of Los Angeles versus Hugh Grant, film actor of England.

Have you anything to say in your defence in regard to this charge of lewd behaviour in a motor vehicle, Mr Grant?

Yes, Your Honour. Although I am better known for my other career I am, like Rowan Atkinson, a part-time motoring journalist. I test cars, Sir. It is necessary for me to be able to inform my readership of the vehicle's qualities in every respect.

But Mr Grant, the prosecutor gives me to understand that it was not the qualities of the car you were testing, but the qualities of something else altogether. And quite Divine it was, too, apparently.

Your Honour, you must understand that it is sometimes necessary to simulate certain conditions in order to properly test certain aspects of a car. That is what I and my assistant were doing when rudely interrupted by the officers. First, Sir, there was the car's demisting ability. Convertibles tend to mist up very badly. So my assistant and I simulated a misting situation, after which I had intended to turn on the air conditioning to see how quickly it cleared. Misting simulations require an activity that will create mist, Sir. The more thorough motoring writers do it all the time.

I see, Mr Grant. But why is it necessary for you to carry out this misting exercise with your trousers round your ankles? Your trousers were round your ankles, were they not?

Yes, Sir. They were. That is another test that we do. We need to assess the breathing qualities of the upholstery material and what it feels like to the touch. My readers can be found living in all kinds of climatic regions from searing deserts to the sub-arctic. Some will be driving with skimpy shorts and mini-dresses, with much flesh in contact with the seat. Others will be driving fully clothed. I need to know if human skin sticks unpleasantly to seats. When you think about it, Sir, the buttocks are a major sensory organ in the relationship between a person and a car. There is more buttock between you and a car than almost anything else. Driving a fine car with bare buttocks sends the motoring writer many interesting messages . . .

But Mr Grant, you were seen to be caressing the nylon-stockinged legs of your so-called assistant. Of course, you will have an explanation of why a motoring writer needs to do this.

Yes, Sir. Many cars will give you a static electric shock when you get out. This is an extraordinarily annoying problem for many owners. The static is generated by nylon and other synthetic materials in clothes and shoes. Some car makers now claim that they have static earthing circuits in the interior door pulls that de-charge you before you get out. It is our task, Sir, to generate some static electricity by rubbing nylon, then to get out of the car and see if we get zapped.

Mr Grant, your assistant's head was out of view, down low in the car somewhere.

Yes, Sir. She was measuring rear passenger leg room for my report.

Mr Grant, I am not going to even bother asking you why your assistant needed to re-apply her lipstick as the officers approached. I fear you will tell me that this was a check on the car's vanity mirrors. I am going to cut you short the way the officers almost did and dismiss the charge. I'm retiring from the Bench at the end of the month. Are there any vacancies at that magazine you write for?

Those Wonderful
Aussie Tanks

If you have lived in Australia or New Zealand for a reasonable length of time, and if you have followed the fortunes of cars, their designers, their marketers, and their buyers, you cannot have escaped the phenomenon of the large 'Australian' car.

Consider the wide openness of much of Australia. Consider the vast intercity distances. Consider the perception Australians have of themselves as generally tough and no-nonsense people, the way third and fourth generation descendants of pioneers and land-breakers generally do, and you have a psychology that expresses itself in terms of big and brash. You have, in fact, a latter day manifestation of the American psyche.

When this translates into cars, you have a preference and an affection for size. Australians and New Zealanders, from the 1920s to the early 1950s, welcomed large American cars. As the Australasian indigenous motor industry began to bud, it was clear that there was going to be a ready market for a large car.

Not as large, perhaps, as America's Ford V8 Mercuries and Buick Roadmasters, as petrol was not as cheap as in the US and times were still tough following World War II. The tincture of Britishness that remained in the Australian and New Zealand national identities meant we would not go for a complete loss of inhibition, excessively outrageous styling and extraordinarily indulgent bulk the way postwar America did. But yes, size mattered.

Late in 1998, Ford arrested me and flew me from Auckland to Sydney (economy class, I might say) to test drive the new AU Falcon on New South Wales' interior roads prior to the car's public release.

I put my hands up and allowed myself to be handcuffed because the Falcon is a big-selling car in Australia and New Zealand. This car, and the Holden Commodore, are still top sellers, and are today's proof that those early predilections have endured.

Certainly, over the years many buyers have opted for smaller cars. Fuel prices, taxes, traffic congestion, crowded cities, political correctness . . . all have had their influence. But still the big Holdens and Falcons remain hugely successful sellers. The latest model AU Falcon and various mutations of it will be with us for several years to come, given the $100 million investment Ford has put into it.

As an aside to this essay on the very special phenomenon of the Australian car, can I just drop into the conversation that New Zealand and Australian writers frequently join together to test drive Holdens and Falcons, and sometimes other brands. We all know each other and have long ago sorted out most of our tribal and vocabularial differences. We Kiwis have now worked out what an Eggnisher is. It is what you start up when you press the button with the snowdrop or the letters a/c on it.

The Australians have pointed out that those signs in Kiwi pubs saying 'We serve drinks, not drunks' appear to be meaningless when converted to actual New Zealand speech. In the

Kiwi idiom of a feed of fush and chups followed by great sux, we agree the sign is confusing. Of course, they do not realise that the 'great sux' reference has hidden meanings. It houses delights the like of which they would not mock if only they understood.

One Australian motoring journo over a period of a year or so in 1997 and 1998 continued to needle the Kiwis by uttering at every opportunity the words, 'Here come the sheep shaggers.' I am not a large man. I am also a psychologist by qualification. Therefore it is an instructive statement about men, educated men, that this guy stretched me to the point that I announced that I was going to plant him if he made this inane reference once more in our company.

If I had gone ahead and done it, it would have been a personal first. It turned out to be unnecessary. And thus, I am sure, I was spared injury. But if anyone is going to draw you out to perform your personal best, it will probably be an Australian.

Generally, the Australian journos and the Kiwi journos get along together very well, although the Aussies will always group themselves around their own table after dinner, giving the Kiwis the clear message that we are a minor island state like Tasmania. I can cope with that psychologically, given that I am a citizen of the UK, the EC and New Zealand, and have right of entry to Australia. Therefore they know not who they are slighting. I am sure that out of earshot and at some other time, the Kiwis have given as good as they have got. It is inevitable that Australians will see themselves as superior, simply due to the size of their country.

How did I get onto this anyway? We were talking about my being hijacked and abducted from Auckland to Sydney to assay the new AU Falcon, this being a car that will be with us in one form or another well into the new millennium.

The Falcon is an icon in Australia and New Zealand. It is a phenomenon in that it is arguably the only all-Australian car remaining. Nearly 90 per cent of the Falcon's components are made in Australia (alloy wheels and alloy cross members are made in New Zealand). The car is designed largely by Australians for Australians.

Holden has done a very good job over the years of creating the perception that its Commodore range is all Australian, to the extent that most Australians and many New Zealanders fervently believe that to be the case. In fact, the Commodore has always been cloned from cars designed by General Motors' German arm, Adam Opel AG, and sold in Europe as an Opel or in Britain as a Vauxhall.

Holden in Australia has taken the so-called donor car and heavily modified it for Australian conditions, and then manufactured the car in Australia. The VT Commodore, the series that will take Holden perhaps as far as the year 2005, was modelled on the European Opel 2800. But so much modification has been done to it for Australia that the Opel 2800 and the VT Commodore scarcely share a part in common, making the VT Commodore and the various upgrade models that will spin off it more Australian than any Commodore has ever been.

The Ford Falcon began life in late 1959 in the United States as a compact car, giving Ford USA a vehicle to offer customers who could not cope with or did not want the huge Fairlane or Galaxie models. It was almost immediately taken up by Ford Australia and quickly endeared itself to Australians and New Zealanders. When Ford America ceased offering the car, Ford Australia was unwilling to let go of a lucrative niche and a genre that had done good business for the company against its arch rival, General Motors (Holden). A decision was made to develop an Australian Ford that would continue the Falcon name and continue to offer Holden some healthy competition.

The 1966 Falcon XR was the first Falcon to have significant Australian input. The whale-shaped XA Series introduced in 1972 was the first fully Australian-designed Falcon. The next major change of shape came in 1979 with the squared-off XD, which almost gave the two-fingered salute to the curved look.

Each new model Falcon sent waves of excitement and loyalty through the Australian automotive psyche.

And so in the '60s and '70s a three-way battle ensued, the third contestant being Chrysler, which had Australianised a design from its Plymouth Division in Michigan, in the form of the Valiant.

The Valiant was first shown in the United States towards the end of 1959. Strangely enough, the car was to be called the Falcon. At the last minute, it was learned that Ford had registered that name, so a hasty naming competition was held among Chrysler staff. The car was to have looked like the Renault Dauphine, with generous curvaceousness and a rear engine of 'slant four' design. The 'slant' reference describes the way the engine was tipped to one side of the perpendicular axis so that the engine bay did not need to be tall. Chrysler got increasingly icy feet about the concept, quickly added two more cylinders to the slant four engine, dropped the curves and shifted the engine up front. As a compact car to place before the American people, this felt a much more comfortable format.

Two hundred Valiants were trialled as New York taxis. Mysteriously, when they had been idling for a few minutes, they stopped dead. No amount of effort appeared to be able to restart them. The expired ones were towed away to some kind of Chrysler Casualty Clearing Station, where it was found that the spark plugs were soaked in oil. This was traced to a piston ring fault, and a new ring was quickly designed.

By 1962 the car was well sorted out and it went into production in Australia with a 3.7-litre slant six engine. A year later, a model called the AP5 was introduced, the AP standing for 'Australian Production'. Shortly after there followed a V8 variant and a station wagon body.

The model was so well received in Australia that Chrysler could not meet demand. It had a revolutionary automatic gear selector which was a row of silver buttons on the dashboard. The AP6 that followed saw the push buttons disappear in favour of a column-mounted selector. But the car remained popular and in 1966 the VC model appeared with a new nose and tail grafted onto the old cabin. Various models succeeded it, and the Valiant held its own in the three-way battle of the big car makers that was fought out on Australian turf in the '60s and '70s.

Holden got its start in 1944. A team of Australian and American designers began work in Detroit on what was to be the first Australian-built mass production car. It would be assembled by a company called Holden's, a Melbourne firm which built bodies to be fitted to imported chassis. The company was acquired by General Motors in 1931 and was known as General Motors Holden's.

In December 1946, the entire team set sail from North America on the liner *Wanganella*. Australia-bound, they numbered 86 when family members were taken into account. On board were engines, mechanical parts, drawings, jigs, tools, even entire cars. From these, at the Holden works at Fishermen's Bend in Melbourne, an entirely Australian-made car was to be crafted.

From that point, all kinds of arguments and stand-offs broke out between Detroit and Melbourne. GM in Detroit had never been keen on the idea of an Australian car anyway, but much persuasion by GMH had seen them cave in. GM had financed the development of the chassis and engine, but GMH would have to raise its own capital in Australia for the styling and body development. The Commonwealth Bank and the Bank of Adelaide offered to fund this project to the tune of three million pounds, and did so. Melbourne put up drawings for Detroit's approval of a very pretty, modernistic car, with the mudguards flared into the bodywork. Detroit rejected it, wanting more conservative styling with the old-fashioned and prominently separate mudguards that survived on some cars of the day.

There were sackings and resignations and angry memos. In late 1948, the car that was to go into production was shown to a small group from the press. Production began shortly after. The car looked far more antiquated than it needed to, but it was a compromise between the wishes of Detroit and those of Melbourne that at least meant an all-Australian-built car could proceed.

Holden cars were snapped up by the Australian public. It was three years before initial demand was met and cars could be made available to New Zealand.

By the late 1960s, in the Holden camp stood the Belmonts and Kingswoods, later to be supplanted by the Commodore. Ford had its Falcon and Chrysler its Valiant. All offered large six-cylinder in-line engines, with V8 options at the top end of the range. All offered station wagon options. Various two-door hard-top versions with loud stripes and lots of testosterone came and went, as did high-performance specials. Australians developed a rivalry that was embodied in their cars. You were either a Holden, Ford or Chrysler man, or the girlfriend, wife, sister or mother of one. Some of this oddly directed energy, this strange sense of automotively inspired identity, inevitably spilled over into New Zealand.

And so you went to Bathurst or Pukekohe and you cheered for your brand.

Leyland Australia, an offshoot of the British giant, yearned to be invited to the party and began hurriedly designing six-cylinder cars. The Kimberley and the Tasman were box-like front-wheel-driven offshoots of the British Austin 1800 Land Crab. They looked god-awful, were not as big as the three Aussie tanks, and were not as reliable either. Most of all, they were not 'blokish' enough for the antipodeans of those times. So Leyland Australia took the bit firmly between the teeth and in 1973 presented Australia with a truly huge and grunty-looking car, the P76. This magnificent looking creation made Australians and New Zealanders look twice at the languishing Anglo-Australian marque. The P76 was a top effort. It offered a choice of a 2.6-litre six-cylinder cast-iron engine developed from the 2.2-litre unit in the Kimberley, or a 4.4-litre all-alloy V8 developed from that used in the Range Rover and Rover V8 saloon cars, Rover being a related company.

But sadly the damage that had been done to Leyland Australia by earlier cars that did not inspire had become more or less terminal. A few quality and reliability problems with the P76 arose and were less than helpful. Before the P76 really had a chance to rebuild Leyland Australia's credibility, the decision was made to close the company down. Seventeen thousand units had been built and there were plans for a coupe, a utility and a station wagon, some of which reached prototype stage. Sadly, by the end of 1974, the P76 was history. And Australians and New Zealanders went back to cheering for Holden, Ford or Chrysler.

The next one to pull out was Chrysler, which in the second half of the 1970s began to experience difficulties on its US home markets. With the world car industry also having been hit by the first of the oil shocks, Chrysler's head office in the United States decided that the organisation should withdraw from several overseas markets and concentrate on its core business in the States. By late 1978 or early 1979, the last new Chrysler Valiants had been sold. The car had been consigned to history.

This left the big car territory to Ford and Holden. Some time later, Ford decided to cease offering a V8 engine option, but then reversed that decision. But the volume business is in the six-cylinder cars and station wagons, and so the pair have fought it out ever since. One brand would surge ahead, then the other. One would get left behind on technology such as airbags or independent rear suspension, then the other would get left behind on something else.

The Japanese came along in the '90s to try to carve out some of the Australian market for themselves, with cars such as the big Mitsubishi Diamante and the Toyota Camry. Both have done very well in the trans-Tasman markets. But in that large car arena, it is the release of a new Holden Commodore or a Ford

Falcon that is still guaranteed to get a spot on the six o'clock news on most Australian TV networks. That is how nationalistic and traditionalistic Australians remain.

I cannot see anything greatly wrong in this. If some part of your perception of national pride is somehow expressed in a product that is built in your country and which is used by millions of your citizens daily, is there something fundamentally simplistic or uncultured about you? Can anyone really say that this particular form of worship lacks any spiritual values or philosophical depth?

Could not the opposite be the case, whereby the worshipper or follower is actually worshipping and following something tangible that is highly relevant to his or her daily life? Not all religions could make such a claim.

Having said that, no-one gets up my snorer more quickly than someone at a party who collects MGs or Monaros, and on learning that one is a so-called motoring writer, pins one to the wall and extemporises for four hours on the subject.

Ah, Welcome Mr Gill San

I am yet to meet a Japanese who can speak no English at all. I guess there may be some. But my understanding is that their education system has turned English into a compulsory subject because the Japanese economy has long depended on dealing with markets where English is the principal language. A Japanese will see you looking at a guide book or a map in a Tokyo street and will come up and ask if they can help. They just love to practise their English.

They speak English considerably better than foreign motoring writers speak Japanese, but they do not always get it exactly right. On one occasion a Japanese project engineer was asking New Zealand motoring writers what they thought of their test drive in his company's then-new Subaru WRX. *New Zealand Autocar* publisher and former racing driver Mark Petch said, 'The gear change feels very rubbery.'

At which the Japanese engineer broke out in a broad smile and said: 'Aaah so. Frank you for kind compriment Meestar Petch. But we think all of car wery rubbery. Subaru WRX is a wery rubbery car.'

I was also intrigued some years ago by a Toyota handbook that said: 'Please do not force radio control with violence for it may be broken with damage.'

I am also the last to criticise a nation that taught the rest of the world how to design and build vehicles. Henry Ford takes the credit for the introduction of mass production and the constantly moving production line. But the postwar Japanese deserve the credit for building cars that were generous with their features and that were built perfectly. The Europeans, the Americans and the British all grudgingly had to admit in the 1970s and 1980s that they had taken a lesson from the Japanese and ceased building cars that leaked, that had poor panel-fit, weak electrical systems and untidy welding. South Korea's car industry now models itself on that of Japan and is emerging as a powerful world force. There are going to be some winners and losers, though, because the world's capacity to buy new cars in the numbers that they are being produced globally is limited.

I would hate to think where the global car industry would be now if Japan had not played the part it did in reforming it. I have a feeling we would not be driving the quality vehicles that we have today.

I read somewhere that Bill Gates of Microsoft said that if the car industry had taken a lesson from the computer industry, we would now all be driving $25 intelligent cars. I cannot be sure if he really did say that, but he was definitely quoted along those lines. Various people in the world motor industry had plenty to say in reply. I wrote a few lines for my readers at the time which went thus:

There is a document rampaging around on the Internet about how Bill Gates claimed that if the motor industry was as smart as the computer industry, we would all be driving around in highly intelligent cars priced at $25. Which seems to me to be $170 cheaper than Windows 98. A senior motor industry person is said to have put

Gates well-and-truly in his place with a number of rejoinders. Every second newspaper and radio station has retailed the Internet document. Not into regurgitating the Net to readers who pay good money for original material, this writer would like to add a few points of his own. So, I have just upgraded to the Microsoft 2-litre Fiasco GLXi WinCar98. It looks like a good car. But it won't start. It tells me that there is a serious and unrecoverable engine error. Parts of the car may have been lost. Any unsaved parts will be definitely lost and irretrievable. Then it has the gall to make me agree to say 'OK' when things are far from OK, before it will let me out of the vehicle to hail a cab. You have just had a serious accident, the airbags failed to deploy and you might die. OK? No, it is not OK, thank you very much. But you have to say it is OK before the machine will do anything else. Anyway, so my Microsoft car is now re-booted and is back on the road. I exceed the speed limit. I get a message that says this car has just performed an illegal act and will be shut down. If the problem persists, I must contact a Microsoft service agent. I get a $150-per-hour propeller-head person with major acne, halitosis like napalm, and Coke bottle glasses to bring the car back to life. I have just turned into a side road in my Microsoft 2-litre Fiasco GLXi WinCar98 with tinted 'Windows'. Now I get a message that says 'WinCar98 does not recognise this command. Are you sure you want to take this road? For Help press F11. OK?' I am sick of all this and decide to junk the thing. So I flick it into the recycle bin. Still it tries desperately to stay in my life and in my face. It asks, 'Are you sure you wish to delete WinCar 98?' Never have I pressed the 'Yes' command with such surety, such conviction. And just when I thought I had finally got rid of the 2-litre Microsoft Fiasco WinCar98 completely, two days later I find that the bloody thing has turned up back in my garage.

Returning momentarily to those motor industry saviours, the Japanese, I have always been impressed with their openness with journalists. They will let you inspect all kinds of processes and procedures and go to major expense and effort so that you can do so.

Recently I was in Japan with a group of journalists, again via five-star business class courtesy of Honda. Part of our itinerary was a visit to a research and development centre to see some of the work they were doing on both active and passive safety systems, especially airbags. We arrived at the facility on the Honda-arranged bus, complete with tassled curtains and mah-jong tables. There, flying on the flagpole outside the building, was the New Zealand flag. Whenever you are making an official visit to a Japanese company, you will find the flag of your nation flying on a pole outside, and as often as not, there will be a sign in the foyer welcoming you by name. And on this day, they took a brand new Civic out of stock and lined it up ready to crash against the wall for our pleasure and edification. This would show us how the airbags deployed.

Now, I am aware that in biblical days the fatted lamb was killed when the prodigal son decided he might look up his old folks. I am aware that in times past, Eskimos were reputed to offer their wives to help warm guests to the igloo.

But this 'kill a car for the guests' idea seemed to be wantonly sacrificial in the extreme. 'Hey, Sakimoto. The Kiwi journalists have arrived. Fetch out a sacrificial Civic in their honour.'

They proceeded to do just that. A new Civic was wheeled out, put on the railway track that propels sacrificial cars against the wall, and duly sacrificed. I cried myself to sleep for a week.

The only thing I learned from all this was that the airbags in Civics seem to work well, but the gas in them smells appalling. But I guess you don't care about that so much after an airbag has saved your life. A bad smell is not a big issue in that situation.

The Japanese engineers seemed very pleased with themselves and beamed all over the dust that settled around their wrecked car, and we could do little other than mount a round of applause. The Japanese like applause and it is, in fact, used a lot in business. A Japanese businessman being introduced to other people at a meeting will invariably be given a round of applause. And according to Japanese tradition, no speaker goes without a round of applause when they are introduced to the audience, and again at the conclusion of their speech. It doesn't matter that the speaker was so boring you went into a week-long deep sleep. The Japanese who were still awake when the speech concluded would have clapped. Generally, it is a weak, insipid sort of effort, a bit like that which is produced when people are trying to clap with a glass or cup in one hand. But it is applause nevertheless. And it is such an important part of life that the Japanese car company Daihatsu named a car after it.

After we had watched the Civic being sacrificed, I was subjected to one of the weirdest experiences of my life. The Honda people toured us through the crash dummy store. Honestly, it was like going through an apartment block inhabited by real people. This was where the crash dummies lived and chatted and waited until their next assignment.

There were baby crash dummies, Mummy crash dummies, Daddy crash dummies. This was a haunting experience. Scores of surrogate humanity with eyes, skulls, hairdos, in some cases breasts, looked at you as you toured among the racks that they reclined upon, awaiting their next job.

They even had good clothes on. Well, good in my world. Perhaps not so good at op-shops. You felt such an empathy with them that you wondered if they had sex lives and dreams and aspirations. It was such a left-field experience that you felt you heard conversations between them.

'Lotty, my dear old crash dummy. I was looking for you in

the Concussion Club last night. I was wanting to talk to you about that Internet site I have discovered about premature expiration. But then I heard that the company president took you out of the crash testing programme for 24 hours and sent for you last night. I know how CEOs call down to the Crash Dummy Department when they are angry and need to stick pins or other things into something. I was worried about you, Lotty. I trust and hope that he was gentle. I trust and hope that side impact was not on his mind.'

'Oh, my dear Stephan, you are so kind. Let me assure you that this time he only wanted to ask me if I would sit atop the company Christmas tree again this year. As a dummy, you see, I am not supposed to feel the pain of the impalement. How about you, my dear Stephan. What sort of a day have you had?'

'Well, Lotty, we finally got through the Civic Moose testing programme. I had to put up with twenty airbag deployments. So, as you can imagine, I will have a headache tonight, my dear Lotty.'

'That's OK, Stephan, my good friend. I understand. There is nothing so bad as a headache. As you know, I began as a panty-hose model in a department store. I know about headaches. I spent the day surrounded by teenage girls with metal rings in every orifice, examining my Lycra content. My dear Stephan, they had so many metal rings in so many orifices, that I can only imagine that a man like yourself would think he was making love to a Mitre 10 store.'

'We should not complain so much, my dear Lotty. Life is not so bad, compared to that of our human clones. Unlike them, at least we can say that we start every day with a bang.'

And I had not taken a single drop of sake.

It was the accident from hell, even though nobody seemed to be hurt. The Auckland motorway was wet and bleak. It was a six-car nose-to-tail shunt. I came very close to making it seven. But I was saved by the good offices of ABS. Funny term, that, 'Good offices.' A friend of mine in the motor trade who is given to completely innocent malapropisms phoned me recently and said: 'Peter, I would like to use your good orifices to help me with something.' My cheeks froze. All four of them.

Anyway, it seemed that no-one was hurt in this six-car mating ritual. The occupants had gathered on the shoulder of the motorway and were hurling all kinds of accusations and insults at each other. A Maori man was giving an Asian woman a fairly sharp lesson in culture.

'Don't you know that this road and all roads and all lands belong to Maori? You must use the roads with respect. You must have been speeding and travelling too close to the back of my vehicle. You have offended my culture and smashed the back of my Hi Ace.'

The little Asian lady was tearful in her reply.

'I not go too fast. Asian do not drive fast. Policeman stop me with radar yesterday. He say that radar reading said I going backwards.' She surveyed the sad remains of the grille of her E Class Benz. A sad whiff of steam floated solemnly upwards, engulfing the three-pointed star of Stuttgart.

Meanwhile, a European woman with hirsute legs, a bone necklace and an All Blacks haircut was berating a guy in Versace jeans, a Country Road tartan shirt, Lumberjack boots and a five o'clock shadow.

'This is an outrage against my rights as a woman. You have violated me by running your macho male symbol right up the back of my womanhood. This is typical of the attitude of today's male.'

His ageing BMW Five Series had mounted her tiny Japanese four-wheel-drive.

Strangely, the guy kept uttering, 'Please hold. Please hold.' I could not understand what he meant by that. He seemed to be in the grip of some kind of delirium. The hirsute one was just shaping up to thump him when another woman intervened. The cursing feminist backed off, belched loudly, and tottered off to pick up the spare wheel of her minute four-wheel-drive vehicle, which had sheared off the rear in the crash. She lifted it with one finger and hurled it onto the back seat.

The woman who had intervened seemed a pleasant young blonde who, unlike the other one, knew about those dainty little razor blades with the pink tops that often come attached to a quiver of yellow-topped blades for men. The gases that rose from her perfume rolled across all eight lanes of the motorway. You will have met women who seem to feel the need to fumigate the entire world as they move around in it. In this case, had she applied any more scent, the traffic police would have needed to put out fog warning signs.

I sensed that she was somehow connected to the BMW guy, who was still muttering, 'Please hold. Please hold,' as he contemplated his now-corrugated Bavarian conveyance. He was quite well-spoken, but his voice had that edge that suggests the existence of a long broom handle lodged in a very inconvenient place. A sort of cabin steward voice, if you know what I mean.

'He's my boyfriend,' volunteered the gas cloud. 'I was in his car when all this happened. He was pointing out a billboard for an auto-electrical service that said if your battery's flat call 0800 JUMPME, when all of a sudden we were right on top of this insect of a Japanese Jeep.'

'Careful,' I said. 'There may be lawyers about. I have had letters in the past from Chrysler saying that the legal right to the use of the word Jeep belongs to them. They reserve the right to sue anyone who uses it in association with another brand. Why does your boyfriend keep repeating the phrase "please hold"?'

'Oh, he's the Call Minder man that you hear answering phones when no-one is available to answer them personally. The first time we were in bed together and getting passionate he suddenly went into that "please hold" routine. Another time when I went round to his house, he opened the door and said "you are in a priority queue" and then began to hum "Home on the Range". The relationship has become a bit of a strain. I don't know how long it's going to last. For instance, once when we were on the very precipice of passion he suddenly said "for more options press one".'

The crowd were still slugging it out on the side of the road. In the distance I heard the faint whoop of a siren. A professional was on the way to take over this veritable psychiatric ward. I gave the gas cloud my card in case she should need some counselling at a later date.

And if I needed any reminding that the world had gone mad, just then a truck whisked by. On the back was a sign that said, 'If you have any comments about the operation of this vehicle, dial 0800 EATSHITE'.

Our Journey Ends —
Where To From Here?

Where will the future take us? On this subject, the major car manufacturers and technical universities of the world have been generous in sharing their ideas, and in return, have taken some of mine.

In Australia and New Zealand we are lucky. Our population numbers per available square kilometre of territory are still extraordinarily low by world standards for places of temperate climate. I know that it may not feel that way at times, as you struggle to get from North Sydney to Central, or from Auckland's North Shore to the CBD. The same frustrations, I know, are played out daily in Brisbane, Melbourne, Adelaide, Perth, Wellington and Christchurch. And doubtless a few other places, too.

As they fume and curse in never-ending gridlock, some shave, some put on make-up (the women too), some pick their noses, some try to read the paper. Many make phone calls. A woman who for some reason seems to get behind me every day in the Auckland melee, sits high, wide and handsome in her Range Rover and eats from a bowl. I presume it is breakfast cereal.

Here in Australasia, we will be among the last to come under pressure to make drastic changes to the way we use cars in our lives. Most of us live near the coast. Manageable population numbers, strong and cleansing coastal winds that carry away emissions in many of our cities, and a rebellious nature derived from convict and pioneering roots, mean that we do not accept change meekly. But in the northern hemisphere, things are changing apace. There, the concept that a car, your car, is your passport to complete independence and freedom is disappearing. In some countries, sensors in the road detect the passing of your car and send you a bill for the use of that road. It will be a little while yet before this is a big deal in your life or mine, as a citizen of Australia or New Zealand, although electronic billing as a replacement for manual collection of tolls has begun in a very few places in Australia.

In late 1998 I drove north out of Sydney at the wheel of a brand new AU Falcon, at the time not yet seen by the Australian public, on my way to test it on the interior roads of New South Wales. A toll road that I used was in the process of switching to offering regular users the option of automatic electronic billing. It was the first time I had seen this in our part of the world. I paid in the old time-honoured Australian way, by hurling coins into one of those large wok-like arrangements at the toll gate. But regular commuters can have their cars fitted with the necessary sensors that allow them to avoid queues at toll gates, and instead use a special fast lane through the toll barriers.

Your partner sees the bill and asks what you were doing way out there on that night. You reply quite legitimately that John has got this thing about holding his sales review meetings 30 km out of town at 11 p.m.

Already, in New Zealand, some trucks are being tracked by

satellite in order that they can be charged for road use, as an alternative to using a hub-mounted distance meter for the calculation of dues. One day we will see Global Positioning System tracking of our car movements. We may be charged for the roads that we have used. The vehicle we drive may be one that employs a small petrol engine and an electric one working together. The petrol engine will drive us up hills and do the hard tasks. Coasting down again, power will be generated for the batteries that drive the electric engine.

I invite you as an Aus or a Kiwi to stand out in the freshening wind, and ask yourself if this is what you want. You have lived cars. For some of us, there have been friends who have died in them. For most of us, life continues to revolve around them. Retailing and merchandising are all organised around the assumption that most shoppers will arrive by car. Billions of dollars have been spent on commercial real estate, based on the premise that those seeking goods and services will travel by car. If the car were to be outlawed tomorrow, half the globe would be covered with inappropriate, unsuitable, nigh on useless shops, malls, movie multiplexes, fast food places and service stations.

But how long can we go on saying to ourselves, to society and to government that cars and driving as they are today will remain our right for decades forward, while cities come to a halt daily under a cloud of toxic smog?

In my view, the answer is that the car will be with us for a very long time yet. Our guarantee of that is that no government would have the political bravery to cast all that real estate into disuse. And anyway, politicians themselves would be inconvenienced, which provides an even greater guarantee that it will not happen.

Instead, cars will change. They already are changing. Almost every major manufacturer is now in a position to offer a so-called hybrid car. It will run on battery electricity for some of the time, using its small petrol engine to keep it mobile should the battery run down before the end of the journey. This will drastically reduce pollution and lower the demand for fossil fuels.

Pure electric cars, and I have driven several lately, are now becoming impressively powerful and the distance that they can travel on one overnight recharge is extending into the realm of being practical and worthwhile.

In major metropoli where roads are continually choked, increasing numbers of toll roads will be employed. Travelling on them at peak times will cost dearly. For off-peak travel, there will be substantial discounts.

I know that most of this does not sound like fun. But has driving in a big city ever been fun?

Epilogue

I try not to lose sight of the fact that during my ten times round the clock I have enjoyed enormous privilege. Money, no. But privilege yes. We started this journey with my mentioning to you that at about the time of celebrating my thirtieth year and millionth kilometre as a motoring writer, I drove the most expensive production car ever entrusted to me. It was a half-million-dollar Rolls-Royce Silver Seraph. My friend Roger Bhatnagar has since advised me that this record will soon be broken. He has for some time owned a McLaren F1 valued at somewhere around $2 million. And he wants me to drive it.

It looks as though I am about to start my eleventh traverse of the clock. And I will do so in fine style.

Thanks for riding with me on this journey. I trust that during the time that you have wasted with me you were able to record anything that was any good on TV.

So, happy driving. And try not to brake at the apex.